Chekhov's

Uncle Vania and *The Wood Demon*

Donald Rayfield

Bristol Classical Press
Critical Studies in Russian Literature

This edition first published in 1995 by
Bristol Classical Press
an imprint of
Bloomsbury Academic
Bloomsbury Publishing Plc
36 Soho Square,
London W1D 3QY

© 1995 by Donald Rayfield

CIP records for this book are available from the
British Library and the Library of Congress

ISBN 978-1-85399-405-0

www.bloomsburyacademic.com

Contents

Acknowledgements

The original research for this study could not have been conducted without the help of Alevtina Pavlovna Kuzicheva of the Chekhov commission of the Russian Academy of Sciences, thanks to whom I was able to use the full resources of the Manuscript Section of the Russian State Library, the Museum of the Moscow Arts Theatre (MKhaT) &c., and through whom I met a great number of Chekhovists and *teatraly*, in Sumy, Taganrog and Yalta as well as other cities, who have enriched my knowledge greatly.

The germ of this book, however, lies in an undergraduate essay by Alan Gale (like many London taxi-cab drivers, a well-trained and articulate thinker) who convinced me that a reading of *The Wood Demon* was an essential enhancement in understanding *Uncle Vania*.

A grant from the British Academy helped to finance my research: I express my thanks.

Part One

Introduction: The Genesis of *The Wood Demon*

Why write a study combining two plays, one world famous, the other known to only a few? *Uncle Vania*, from its first publication and performances in 1897, was recognised as a play of genius and established Chekhov's reputation as the greatest living playwright in Russia: in the few remaining years of Chekhov's lifetime it was printed in dozens of editions and hundreds of thousands of copies. *The Wood Demon* survived only a handful of performances at the end of December 1889 and was generally condemned by the audience, critics and actors as an unstageable and incompetent play: Chekhov was urged by all to limit himself to narrative prose. The play was published in August 1890 only in a lithograph reproduction, 110 copies, of a fair-copy version written out by various members of the actor Svobodin's family, and it lay unprinted until seven years after the author's death. Opinion on the two plays' merits has changed little since then: exceptions, such as Tolstoy's disgust at the triviality of *Uncle Vania* or Michael Frayn's defence of the dramatic potential of *The Wood Demon*, are voices crying in the wilderness.

This study sets out to account for, even modify, but not to revolutionise opinion. Nevertheless, *The Wood Demon* is important for several reasons: it shows Chekhov experimenting, overturning many of the theatrical conventions of his day in the search for a new drama, an experiment he was to repeat more recklessly in *The Seagull* in 1895; as literary prose half-converted into drama, *The Wood Demon* tells us much about his evolution as a story writer; as almost the only major work Chekhov wrote which ends with an upbeat affirmative tone, it is a remarkable anomaly. Above all, it is virtually the same play as *Uncle Vania*, for about two-thirds of *The Wood Demon* is to be found in *Uncle Vania*, and the cast list of *Uncle Vania*, with one exception, is all to be found in *The Wood Demon*. A study of the two shows how a bad play can, over eight years, by radical revision, ruthless cuts, cautious additions, be converted into a great play. A comparison of the two texts tells us not only how Chekhov found himself as a dramatist (*Uncle Vania* is the model for the greatest plays, for *Three Sisters* and *The Cherry Orchard*) it is a practical lesson in the playwright's art, enormously instructive to any novice in search of the secrets of the technical mastery.

The strangeness of *The Wood Demon* would be more explicable were it Chekhov's first full-length play, but it is not. Chekhov had discarded the play which he probably wrote around 1883 and which is generally known as *Platonov*:[1] it has the crowded cast, the testing length, the uncertain lunges from pathos to farce, the setting of a provincial estate whose peace is threatened by the summer visitors and by the characters' moral and financial fecklessness. Yet, as Michael Frayn's *Wild Honey* shows, *Platonov* can be cut into an enthralling, if ludicrous, drama. Chekhov's only 'legitimate' full-length play before *The Wood Demon* was *Ivanov*. *Ivanov* went through several versions, from comedy to tragedy to drama, between October 1887 and January 1889. It won respectful notices and audiences, if not acclaim or ovations, when performed in Moscow and St Petersburg and when printed in the reputable *Northern Herald*. Chekhov was dismayed (not for the last time) by the inability of the actors and critics to act or understand his central protagonist (Ivanov) who is neither hero nor villain. In vain he drew graphs, trying to show that Ivanov is a case of psychological illness where condemnation is irrelevant: as other dramatists have pointed out, while the madness of Lear or George III is interesting, less maniacal forms, such as depression, lack dramatic potential.

The *Wood Demon* and *Uncle Vania* have in common with *Ivanov* a central character (Voinitsky: Uncle Zhorzh [Georges] or Uncle Vania) whose steadily deepening depression ends in a gunshot-suicide in *The Wood Demon*, and attempted murder in *Uncle Vania*. Likewise, we have a far-sighted outsider in all three plays – a doctor, who makes diagnoses and prognoses, but withholds treatment. But by comparison, *Ivanov* is a conventional play: Acts 2, 3 and 4 end with spectacularly melodramatic confrontations, a hero is seen in thrall to an ineluctable force destroying his will and his moral nature. The play is built on tried and tested foundations: the progress of a moral disease, the conflict of passion and duty. Hence, perhaps, it had a measure of success with the public.

The secret of Chekhov's innovations lies in a desire to confound the established theatre. In Russia theatres were either prestigious, state-subsidised and supervised institutions, or small businesses that were commercial and vulgar, or amateurish and dependent on the enthusiasm of an actor manager. The eccentricities of Chekhov's plays, good or bad, are those of an author asserting himself (for want of a director) against the clichés of professional and amateur actors. The sheer complexity of family relationships, the inconsequentiality of causes and events, the self-indulgent elaborate settings of *The Wood Demon* are due not to ignorance of stage conventions and audience expectations – Chekhov was an inveterate theatre critic – but to contempt for them.

Like all Chekhov's plays, *The Wood Demon* is organically linked with the stories, already written or still to be composed, that Chekhov was preoccupied with. Two groups of story are relevant to *The Wood Demon*. One group are the stories that Chekhov wrote after his first return to the scenery of his childhood, the southern Russian countryside between Voronezh and Taganrog, the former 'Switzerland of the Don' now devastated by the coal-mining and industrialisation wrought by such men as the Welsh engineer Hughes. As a result, stories such as *Panpipes*, *Fortune*, and above all, his deliberate masterpiece, the long prose poem *Steppe*, have to be read as a valedictory celebration of nature, irreversibly destroyed by human myopia and greed. The whole concept of a 'wood demon', a man who frantically rushes about saving forests and repairing the damage to the fabric of ecology, both natural and human, reflects the author dismayed about the disappearance of a childhood idyll. The Wood Demon's speeches, preserved almost intact as Astrov's pleas, reflect the authorial persona of the stories of 1887 and 1888. The other stories relevant to *The Wood Demon* are stories of alienation, the most notable being *A Dreary Story*, which we shall study in more detail as part of the play's literary context. Suffice it to say that Chekhov worked on *A Dreary Story* at the same time as *The Wood Demon* and that the tragic first-person story and the ruthless comedy share not only the central figure of the elderly professor tormenting himself and his family, but also many scenes and images.

The immediate progenitor of *The Wood Demon*, however, must be seen as not Chekhov the story-writer, but Aleksei Sergeevich Suvorin (1834-1912), the Maecenas and commissioning editor. Suvorin was editor and owner of Russia's most powerful newspaper, the right-wing St Petersburg *New Times*. He was a major publisher and his family controlled Russia's station bookstalls. A powerful influence in St Petersburg's theatres, he was also a theatre critic, playwright (both historical dramas and farces), a novelist and political commentator. His own writing was polished, craftsmanlike, but trivial and sensational. Nevertheless, Suvorin was a commercial and political genius. A melancholy man who tyrannised his sons (one committed suicide), a womaniser, particularly with actresses, he recognised Chekhov's importance in 1886 and secured him as a regular contributor to the twice-weekly literary supplements of his newspaper. When in Spring 1888 he invited Chekhov to Petersburg to stay with him and his young second wife, a business relationship turned into a friendship as improbable as, say, a union of Harold Pinter and Rupert Murdoch, and as ominous as the association of Faust and Mephistopheles. The friendship was deplored by most of Chekhov's friends (with the notable exception of actresses who found both men's charm perfectly explicable). Chekhov deplored Suvorin's political stance, especially his anti-semitism, but the father-figure Suvorin became his closest friend for life (despite a breach at the end of the 1890s over the Dreyfus affair). Within weeks of Chekhov's death, Suvorin cannily repossessed all his several hundred letters to Chekhov – what made him so fascinating is now harder to guess. But Chekhov's many letters to Suvorin and his many remarks about him show an unbounded admiration. Suvorin, like Chekhov, had fought his way to literary prominence from humble provincial origins, fought depression by endless activity, and like Chekhov he veered from a puritanical disgust with the world to hedonistic enjoyment of Bohemian female company.[2]

To his dismay, Suvorin saw himself and his wife portrayed in the play as the cantankerous professor married to a much younger woman, who is desirable and deplorably idle. But he is there more fundamentally as co-author. The first fruit of friendship with his publisher was Chekhov's unique desire to collaborate – he would never attempt to do so again, unless we consider his unrealised plans to write a libretto for Tchaikovsky as collaboration – on a work in which Suvorin would be chiefly responsible for certain plot lines, characters, speeches and even whole acts. Presumably Chekhov relied on Suvorin's experience in stagecraft to give a framework to his own psychological subtleties and radical vision of nature, to make a marriage of conventions and the unconventional. How much the original cast list and the situation Chekhov sketched out are borrowed from Suvorin is not clear, but the basic family situation of the original outline for the play reflects Suvorin's presence on two levels, the marital and father–son relationships in Suvorin's life, and Suvorin's personal preoccupation with titivating sexual incompatibilities.

The desire to write a new 'lyrical play' came in May 1888 in the idyllic setting of Luka, the estate of the Lintvariov family on the river Psiol near Sumy. The river and its watermill, the three Lintvariov sisters and the numerous guests left their mark not only on *The Wood Demon*, but on Chekhov's subsequent plays. July 1888 was an even happier period of incubation. Chekhov spent a month in the Crimea with Suvorin at the latter's new house in Feodosia, where they talked endlessly and Chekhov wrote nothing. But by mid-October, back in Moscow, Chekhov had composed an outline of the play for Suvorin, presumably reflecting what he and the grand old man had talked about and the latter had sketched out. It is worth quoting in full, to show the extraordinary transmutations in the material that would eventually become *Uncle Vania*, and how deeply embedded in the earliest phases of Chekhov's ideas are the 'greenest' passages of the latter play.

> I've received the beginning of the play. Thank you.
> Blagosvetlov will be used complete, as he is. You've done
> him well; he is tiresome and irritating from the moment he
> opens his mouth, and if the audience listens to him for 3-5
> minutes at a time, they'll have just the right impression. The
> spectator will think: 'Oh, do shut up, please!' This man, i.e.
> Blagosvetlov, must come over to the spectators both as a

clever, gout-stricken moaner and as a boring piece of music which takes too long to play. I think you'll see how well you have succeeded when I sketch out the first act and send it to you.

In Anuchin I've kept the surname and 'all the essentials', but his conversation has to be lubricated a bit. Anuchin is passive, oily, affectionate, and his speech is also passive, oily, but you make him too jerky and not placid enough. This godfather has to radiate elderly laziness. He can't be bothered listening to Blagosvetlov: instead of arguing, he would rather doze off and listen to stories about Petersburg, the Tsar, literature, science or have a meal in good company....

Let me remind you of the outline of our play:

1) Aleksandr Platonych Blagosvetlov, member of the State Council, order of the White Eagle, has a pension of 7,200 roubles [= £30,000 at today's prices]; is of clerical origin, was taught in priest's college. The position he occupies was won by personal effort. Not a stain on his past. Suffers from gout, rheumatism, insomnia, tinnitus. His real estate came through the dowry. He has a positive outlook. He can't stand mystics, fantasists, cranks, lyrical poets, humbug, he doesn't believe in God and is used to looking at the world from a practical point of view. Practice, not theory – and all the rest is rubbish or quackery.

2) Boris, his student son, a young man, very gentle, very decent, but without the slightest idea of what life is about. He imagined himself to be a populist, tried to dress as a peasant but got himself up like a Turk. He plays the piano very well, sings with feeling, writes plays in secret, falls in love easily, spends masses of money and always talks nonsense. Is a bad student.

3) Blagosvetlov's daughter, but please call her anything but Sasha. I was fed up with that name in *Ivanov*. If the son is Boris, then let the daughter be Nastia. (Let us put up a monument not made by human hand to Boris and Nastia....[3]) Nastia is 23-24. She has had an excellent education and can think.... She is bored with Petersburg and with the country too. She has never been in love. She is idle, loves philosophising, reads books lying down; she wants to get

married just for a change and so as not to be an old maid.
She says she can fall in love only with an interesting man.
She would marry Pushkin or Edison with pleasure, she
would fall in love, but she would marry a good man only out
of boredom; she would respect her husband but love her
children. After seeing and listening to the Wood Demon she
surrenders to the *nec plus ultra* of passion, to the point of
fits, stupid, pointless laughter. The gunpowder dampened by
the Petersburg tundra is drying out in the sun and explodes
with terrible force.... I have thought of a phenomenal declaration of love.

4) Anuchin, the old man. He considers himself to be the
happiest man in the world. His sons have made their way,
his daughters are married and he is as free as the air. He has
never been ill, never been in court, never had medals, forgets
to wind up his watch and is friends with everybody. He dines
well, sleeps excellently, drinks a lot and with no after-effects,
is angry at being old, can't think about death. He used to be
a melancholy moaner, had a bad appetite and was interested
in politics, but he was saved by luck: once, ten years ago, he
found he had to ask everyone at a country council meeting
for forgiveness – afterwards he suddenly felt cheerful, was
hungry and, as a subjective type, sociable to the marrow of
his bones, he concluded that absolute sincerity, like public
penitence, is a cure for all ills. He recommends this cure to
everyone, including Blagosvetlov.

5) Viktor Petrovich Korovin, a landowner of 30-33. The
Wood Demon. A poet, a landscape artist, with a terrific feel
for nature. Once, when he was still a schoolboy, he planted
a birch tree in his back garden; when it turned green and
started to sway in the wind, to rustle and cast a little shade,
his soul was filled with pride; he had helped God to create a
new birch tree, he had seen to it that there was one more tree
on earth! This is the source of his peculiar creativity. He
realises his ideas not on canvas or paper, but on earth, not in
dead paints but with organic materials.... The tree is beautiful, but more than that, it has a right to life, it is as necessary
as water, the sun, the stars. Life on earth is unthinkable
without trees. Trees condition the climate, the climate affects
the character of people etc., etc. There is no civilisation or
happiness if trees crack under the axe, if the climate is harsh

and stale, if people are also harsh and stale.... The future is horrible! Nastia likes him not for his ideas which are alien to her but for his talent, passion, the broad sweep of his idea.... She likes the way his brain sweeps over all Russia and ten centuries ahead. When he runs up to her father in tears, sobbing, implores him not to sell his forests for timber, she laughs loud with delight and happiness that at last she has seen a man she hadn't believe existed when she recognised his features in dreams and novels....

6) Galakhov, the same age as the Wood Demon, but a State Councillor, a very rich man, who served with Skalkovsky. A civil servant to the marrow of his bones and is quite unable to get rid of this aura, for he has inherited it with his flesh and blood from his forefathers.... He wants to live by his heart, but can't. He tries to understand nature and music, but can't. A decent and sincere man who understands that the Wood Demon is higher and openly admits it. He wants to marry for love, thinks he is in love, tries to take a lyrical tone, but it doesn't work. He likes Nastia only because she is a good-looking, clever girl, a good wife, but nothing more.

7) Vasili Gavrilovich Volkov, brother of Blagosvetlov's late wife. He manages the latter's estate (he squandered his own long ago). He regrets not having stolen. He didn't expect his Petersburg relatives to have so little understanding of his merits. They can't and won't understand him and he regrets not having stolen. He drinks Vichy and complains. He emphasises that he's not afraid of generals. He shouts.

8) Liuba, his daughter. She is concerned for earthly things. Chickens, ducks, knives, forks, the cow-shed, the *Niva* prize which has to be framed, feeding visitors, dinners, suppers, tea – that's her sphere. She takes personal offence if anyone pours tea instead of her: 'So I'm not wanted any more in this house, am I?' She doesn't like spendthrifts or idlers. She worships Galakhov for his positive outlook. You haven't presented her right. She should emerge from the depths of the garden, upset and, should raise an outcry: 'How dare Maria and Akulina leave the turkey chicks out all night in the dew?' or something like that. She is always severe. Severe with servants and ducks. Real housewives are never

delighted by their handiwork but on the contrary always try
to argue that their life is like a convict's, God forgive me, I
never get time to rest, everyone sits about doing nothing and
only she, poor woman, is wearing herself to a frazzle.... She
tells Nastia and Boris off for being parasites, but she's afraid
of Blagosvetlov.

9) Semion, a peasant, the Wood Demon's manager.

10) The wanderer Feodosi, an old man of 80, but his hair
is not yet grey. A soldier from Nicholas I's times, served in
the Caucasus and speaks Lezgi. A sanguine type. He loves
stories and cheerful conversation; he bows low to everyone,
kisses their shoulders and kisses the ladies whether they like
it or not. He is a noviciate of the Athos monastery. He has
collected 300,000 roubles over the years and has sent every
penny to the monastery and lives in penury himself. He
tolerates fools and rogues and is unimpressed by rank or
place.

That's the outline for you. By Christmas at the latest you will
have my material for Act 1. I won't touch Blagosvetlov. He
and Galakhov are yours, I renounce them; a good half of
Nastia is yours. I can't cope with her on my own. Boris isn't
important, he's not hard to deal with. The Wood Demon is
mine until Act 4, but in Act 4 he's yours until he chats with
Blagosvetlov. In that chat I shall have to keep to the overall
tone of the figure, the tone which you won't catch.
    The second act (visitors) you also will begin.
    Feodosi is an episodic character, who I think will be
needed: I want the Wood Demon not to be alone on the stage,
so that Blagosvetlov will feel surrounded by cranks. I have
left out of the sketch Mlle. Emilie, an old French lady, who
is also delighted by the Wood Demon. We have to show how
these Wood Demons affect women. Emilie is a nice old lady,
a governess who hasn't lost her spark yet. When she is
excited she mixes French and Russian. She is Blagosvetlov's
patient nurse. She is yours. I am leaving gaps in the first
scene for her [...].

Oddly enough, this plan resembles *Uncle Vania* even more than *The
Wood Demon*: there are only eight main characters, and they include the
professor's nurse. Blagosvetlov's name means 'Good Light', which is only

a step to Serebriakov, 'Silver Man': the professor's humble clerical origin, his diseases, his belief in practice, not theory, his retirement are consistent from this sketch to the final play. Only the negative, even villainous aura is yet to be built up. Viktor Korovin, the Wood Demon, later to be Khrushchev and then Dr Astrov, already has phrases of his speeches, notably the mystical joy of the swaying birch tree. Vasili Volkov in the plan is clearly Voinitsky (Zhorzh in *The Wood Demon*, Vania in *Uncle Vania*): his regret that he never stole from the estate he managed is the germ of the row around which both Acts 3 are to be built. Both Sonia, his sister in the two plays, and Iulia Zheltukhina (in *The Wood Demon*) are to develop from Liuba, Volkov's sister, with her concern for the teapot and the chickens. Nastia (named after Suvorin's young daughter), in love with the Wood Demon, has traits of both Elena and Sonia. One character that was abandoned by the time *The Wood Demon* was being composed is the French governess – she had been borrowed straight from life, for Mlle Emilie Bijon was governess to the Suvorin family. (Then just 30, she was particularly fond of Chekhov, with whom she maintained a correspondence and for whom she sometimes put on an Alsatian girl's costume.)

Suvorin must be seen as the co-begetter, if not the co-author of the play, for he soon rejected the idea of collaboration. Right until autumn Chekhov tried to retain him: 'I know very well that *The Wood Demon* is right for a novel. But I haven't the strength for a novel.... If I were to write a comedy *The Wood Demon*, my first concern would be not the actors or the stage, but literary qualities. If the play had literary significance, I'd be grateful for that' (24 x 88). 'Why do you refuse to write *The Wood Demon* together? If the play didn't work or if for any reason you didn't like it, I'd give you my word never to perform or print it.' Whether Suvorin saw the play's intractably un-scenic nature, or whether he was offended by the increasing resemblance of an unpopular, elderly self-made professor with a young second wife to himself, or whether he was overcome by his periodic depression, we don't know: he was adamant.

Suvorin's refusal would have aborted the play, but for an enthusiastic midwife. By Spring 1889 Chekhov was composing *The Wood Demon* in his head: 'Striding during dinner across the room, I composed the first three acts very satisfactorily, and just about sketched the fourth. Act 3 is so full of rows that when you see it you'll say: "This was written by a cunning, merciless person."' The midwife was the actor Pavel Svobodin. He was an enthusiastic reader of Chekhov's prose and, although he criticised the faults of *Ivanov*, he could not believe a Chekhov play could fail. He urged him to produce a play for his benefit performance at the Aleksandrinsky theatre in St Petersburg by October. Svobodin's engaging affection was reciprocated: he was one of the very few people outside the family whom Chekhov addressed as *ty*. Svobodin wrote (2 v 89): 'You call me "demon-tempter",

but you didn't say what you meant by this. But I have to know and tell my
employers straight away what I shall put on for my benefit. Again I ask you
to agree immediately, to give your word, or else to refuse, but to give a
definite answer.' 10 viii 89: 'What has happened to our *Wood Demon*?' 22
xi 89: 'What are you doing to me, you shameless man? How can *The Wood
Demon* come like this? After all you have definitely refused to finish it in
time for this season, and I was forced to think up another play for my benefit
and I chose the *Jacobites* – and now "There will be a Wood Demon!" – well,
the Wood Demon take you, I shall hang myself. If I had your comedy I
wouldn't think about any other. That's why it was especially unforgivable
not to write to me for so long. The only justification you might have is that
you didn't know yourself that you would decide to rest during "an excursion
into Melpomene's province," as you write. In any case, if you were to finish
The Wood Demon early enough for me to perform it, then I would, despite
everything [...] No I'm superstitious and I am afraid of November every
year, that is the month for disasters in my life (I was married on 12
November 1873) and therefore if we don't manage to arrange the benefit in
October, as the director wants, then I won't take it at any price in November
– it is better to have no play at all.' 27 x 89: 'Now on the contrary I am ready
to persuade you to the point of tears to sit down and not leave your desk
until you finish it. Last night I had your letter in which (I hope) you were
lying when you said you had thrown the two acts of *The Wood Demon* into
the river Psiol.... God forbid!!! Have you gone mad, Antoine? Two or three
strokes in a fit of inspiration is all that those two acts lacked, and the two
others would have written themselves [...]'

Svobodin gives us some clues about the evolution of Chekhov's outline
into the play (28 ix 89):

> Well here is the exposition I promised of the content of the
> comedy as I understand it. Professor Z. who thinks he is a
> genius and a man capable of revealing truth to the world, has
> married a young educated girl, who has loved the idea and
> not the man in the professor. The professor's wife has a sister
> – a simple, young, lively person with no pretensions to ideas
> – a girl capable of loving whoever she likes – just that, not
> interested whether he is worthy of her love or has enough
> *ideas*. A certain Y. who has never loved himself and conse-
> quently never known requited love, pesters and bothers the
> wife of the mediocre professor and buzzes in her ears that
> she is putting on an act, that as she is young, beautiful,
> thirsting for real love, she is only deceiving herself and her
> husband the professor, a man who is older, drier and sourer
> than she – that she loves him sincerely: she needs to find a

real outlet for everything that nature gave her, a heart, a soul.... He hints to her that if he isn't what she needs, then there is a real man, the Wood Demon. She half listens to this irritating noise but in any case you can't say his talk doesn't repeat much of what she would dream of alone, with her pillow, confiding her secret dreams to everybody. Meanwhile the sister of the professor's wife and the Wood Demon seem to have taken a fancy to each other, and the professor, as if on purpose, is about to win such a victory in science that his wife, who is now vacillating, is about to believe in the *idea* and reject everything worldly and living for the sake of her ideological love for the supposedly great man of science. At the same time she just does not want to admit or say aloud what she has been nurturing in her soul, that the Wood Demon is better, younger, more talented, nicer than the old mediocre pedant of a professor and she pushes away that 'whiner' who keeps on tempting her, supposing that everything in the world is *idea* and not *life* itself. But all this has lasted only so long as she has noticed and understood that the Wood Demon and her sister love each other, that the Wood Demon is an *idea* that she could possess as she does her husband the professor (as an idea too) and that the Wood Demon is substantially lost to her. Then she becomes human outside any idea and tells her sister: 'Give it to me! I have more rights to him than you – you just chanced on this love, whereas I have nurtured, hidden and suffered it – I have been pretending!' What you can develop on this canvas is not for me to tell you, dear friend. Forgive me for what I've left unclear or omitted – be magnanimous about all the rest.

Chekhov probably disliked this garbled summary, for Svobodin then wrote (29 ix 89):

Dear Antoine, I ask you once more to be kind about my probably disorderly and senseless exposition of *The Wood Demon*, which I hurriedly wrote in yesterday's letter. We really ought to live for two weeks together now, or at least see each other every day – and *The Wood Demon* would just sprout! You would go fully armed after him in the forest and I would part the thorny branches in your path, would clear the trail and the two of us would find him and drag him out by his horns very fast and nothing would prevent us showing him to the Petersburgers on the stage – 'There you are, what

better Wood Demon could you want?' But to do this I ought
to come and see you, not the other way round: the environment here doesn't suit you. They say Schiller when he
worked liked to put rotten apples by him and in the desk,
while you absolutely have to have people singing and making a noise upstairs which Michel is painting the stove tiles
in the Pompeii Kudrino style and for there to be a smell of
Michel's paint as bad as Schiller's rotten apples – well, what
ever the smell to inspire you, write, for the sake of the God
who created the Psiol, write, Antoine! Leave those two acts
as they are and write the two others and quick march here!

What Chekhov thought of this confused résumé of his work we can only
guess. In 1892 the consumptive Svobodin was to collapse and die on stage,
acting a part in Ostrovsky's farce *The Clowns*, and the letters he had received
from Chekhov were lost.

The extraordinary fact is that Chekhov completed *The Wood Demon* by
the end of October 1889. In March he had composed two acts of it in his
mind 'pacing the room from end to end'. In May he had even asked the
Society of Russian Dramatists to include *The Wood Demon* as a comedy in
their catalogue of plays. Then in June all work became impossible: his
brother Nikolai had died a harrowing death in the country near Sumy; in
July Anton fled his grieving family and began a solitary peregrination south,
to Odessa, Yalta; in August he had returned to Sumy to finish his prose poem
to death, the Solomonic first-person narrative *A Dreary Story*. In September
he was back in Moscow: he softened to Svobodin's pleas and even took up
the abandoned play 'with enjoyment'. All October the play was being
copied for the censor and the actors. Chekhov wrote to the actor Lensky (his
lead actor, but soon to be his most severe critic) (6 x 89): 'The play is
finished and is now being written out in a fair copy. If it is any good, then
I am very glad to be of service and shall be extremely flattered if my baby
sees the wings of the Maly theatre.' Svobodin had arranged his benefit
performance for the last auspicious date, 31 October. But no sooner was the
baby born, than it was rejected, exposed on a mountain of critical contempt
that we shall examine when we look at its reception.

The Wood Demon: A Commentary

Before we examine the hostile reception and the theatrical and literary context of *The Wood Demon*, we must take a close look at the text itself to realise what a strange and monstrous play Chekhov had written. We have only the lithographed text to go on as no production notes survive. The only variations are in a prompter's copy, where the few pencilled cuts already point the way to *Uncle Vania*. The producer's heart must have sunk from the moment he saw the cast list, which had inflated to twice the size of the cast sketched by Chekhov in his letter to Suvorin. The family core of characters – the professor (now Serebriakov), his young wife (now Elena Andreevna), his daughter (now Sonia) and his brother-in-law by his first wife (Voinitsky) – remains according to plan (with the addition of his mother-in-law, Voinitsky's mother, Maria Vasilievna). So does the force for disturbance, the outsider, the Wood Demon himself, now Khrushchev. But outsiders – friends and neighbours – now crowd the action. We have not only the rich landowner Zheltukhin, but his sister Iulia and the Orlovskys, father and son, as well as Diadin the owner of the mill. Thus the contrast of stagnant 'residents' or 'family' with 'visitors' or 'outsiders' so typical of a Chekhov play seems unbalanced. There are five 'family', six 'outsiders', not to mention visitors with non-speaking parts and two servants.

The names they bear seem arbitrary, with one outstanding exception, Fiodor Ivanovich Orlovsky, whose characterisation as a swashbuckling, even demonic force, a killer and a seducer is even stronger in the early version of *The Wood Demon* that Chekhov prepared for the censor. The name and patronym Fiodor Ivanovich was in Russian minds inexorably linked with Fiodor Ivanovich Tolstoy, or Tolstoy-Amerikanets, a distant cousin of the writer Lev Tolstoy, and a gambler, womaniser and psychopathic duellist whose murderous exploits in Petersburg, the Aleutian Islands and the Urals form a chapter in Russian urban folklore. There is no doubt that the aura of fear around the younger Orlovsky derives from his being called Fiodor Ivanovich. The woman he pursues and whose beauty causes so much destruction, Elena, is naturally named for Helen of Troy, although the references in Chekhov's play clearly point to Offenbach's *La belle Hélène* rather than to Homer. Perhaps we can find symbolism, too, in the avuncular Diadin [*literally* uncle], or Serebriakov [*literally* man of silver] who turns out to be base metal. Perhaps most striking, however, is the name that Chekhov chose for the victim (and his mother) of the play, Voinitsky. (In *Platonov* he had named the central protagonist family Voinitsev.) The name Egor Voinitsky recalls the traditional name of St George the Dragon Slayer, Egor Voin [*literally*, warrior]. If Chekhov chose the name consciously, then it must be ironically, for this particular St George fails in his attack on the dragon (the Professor) and has no success with the maiden (Elena).[4] Certainly Chekhov uses name symbolism here rather more strongly than he does in any other of his plays, and the connection with names used in earlier plays is clearer. Apart from Voinitsev-Voinitsky, the doctor's first names Mikhail Lvovich recall the priggish doctor Lvov who was the chief antagonist in *Ivanov*.

Subtitled comedy, the play naturally raises expectations of alliances and marriages: but such a number of unattached or semi-detached characters implies too many possible permutations for a normal intrigue. Every character seems doubled, as though Chekhov needed to give them each a confidant(e), or as if he could not decide between two variants: Serebriakov and Orlovsky senior, the Wood Demon and Zheltukhin, Voinitsky and Fiodor Orlovsky junior, Sonia and Iulia are pairs of characters who are all to be fused into single characters when the play is converted into *Uncle Vania*. The stage is crowded with enough characters for a novel. (It is significant that in 1888 and 1889 Chekhov's letters repeatedly mention his longing to write a novel; moreover, in Act 1, Scene 3 Voinitsky, in abusing Serebriakov, says, 'With my powers of observation I ought to write a novel. The plot just asks to be put on paper'.)

Although both *The Wood Demon* and *Uncle Vania* resemble *Platonov* and *Ivanov* in being plays built around a central male protagonist, they are fundamentally different in that the title role is not the sole protagonist: neither the Wood Demon nor Voinitsky are on stage all the time, and very often the audience is preoccupied by the predicament of the second male role (whether Zhorzh Voinitsky or Dr Astrov) or that of a heroine (Sonia) in search of love. The arrival of the antagonist in the form of the professor determines the outcome of several searches. Chekhov has fragmented the central hero for ever.

The diversity of scenes – and this is the last play where Chekhov broke up the flow of each act into conventional scenes – is as bewildering as that of characters: Act 1 is set outdoors on the estate of Leonid and Iulia Zheltukhin, Acts 2 and 3 in the Serebriakov household, Act 4 again outdoors in Diadin's mill. Nevertheless, the play's opening devices could not be more conventional: the two major heroes, the professor and the Wood Demon do not appear until near the end of the Act, Scenes 6 and 7, while the host of minor characters set the scene and expound the plot, or rather the potential for the plot.

Scene 1 opens on a terrace. The secondary characters, the unhappy bachelor

Leonid Zheltukhin and his sister Iulia are waiting for their guests: Professor
Serebriakov, his wife Elena, his daughter Sonia and Voinitsky, his brother-
in-law by his first marriage. Zheltukhin talks of his unrequited love for
Sonia. Gradually the stage is filled. Scene 2 brings in the bland Orlovsky,
Serebriakov's friend and *kum* (the godfather of his daughter Sonia) and the
acrid Voinitsky. Scene 3 adds some silent guests and introduces Diadin, the
spirit of conciliation who is to end as the *deus ex machina* of the play's plot.
At last, in Scene 3, the action begins as Voinitsky cynically sketches
Professor Serebriakov's biography. The first 'problem' that *The Wood
Demon* addresses is the real nature of Serebriakov. If he is the mediocre
charlatan that Voinitsky claims, then how has he made his way from being
the son of a church cantor to holding a chair in St Petersburg? how has he
outshone Don Juan with women and acquired a young second wife in his
dotage? (Note how frequently the distinguished old men of Chekhov's
fiction have fought their way up from lowly clerical origin – a semi-auto-
biographical trait to be found in the professor of medicine in *A Dreary Story*,
and in the bishop in the story of that name [1902].) Like all Chekhov's
problems, and unlike Ibsen's enigmas, the contradiction is not solved by the
text, but left for actor and director. The first wife, Voinitsky's sister Vera
Petrovna, as yet unnamed, 'a beautiful meek creature, as pure as the blue
sky', is a typical touch of the mature Chekhov: a corpse whose presence
haunts the play, but about whom we are to be told tantalisingly little. This
innovation, like the father of the Three Sisters or the heroine's son in *The
Cherry Orchard*, holds the key to the action, whose mainsprings thus remain
locked to the end. Scene 3 adds mystery to the clash of cynicism (Voinitsky)
with the benevolence of the other characters, a benevolence that sometimes
overwhelms the play with its treacliness. Diadin's ludicrously pathetic
life-story can be seen as a parody of Voinitsky's unrequited love (like
Telegin's in the later play) and as a parody takes the sting out of our
compassion for Voinitsky. True, Diadin's loyalty to his unfaithful wife is as
farcical as it is touching, but his absurd sentiments lead only to Orlovsky's
praising him for his fine soul: nobody heeds the moral example. Note,
however, how Orlovsky's criticism, 'You wave your arms about' was
recycled by Chekhov in *The Cherry Orchard* in Trofimov's reproaches to
Lopakhin.

The happy atmosphere is not breached in Scene 4 by the entry of the
aggressive vodka-drinking, philandering Fiodor Orlovsky: he is bathed in
paternal affection and then, in Scene 5, by the friendship of the Zheltukhins.
This scene clearly gave Chekhov some difficulty: in the lithographed
version of the play it is shorter than the version submitted to the censor.
Chekhov cuts Zheltukhin's portrayal of the Wood Demon as a 'mix of satire
and Mephistopheles'. More important, the crucial germ of the plot, the
rumour that Voinitsky is Elena's lover, is more subtly expressed. In the

censor's version no doubt is left in Orlovsky's mind: Zheltukhin says, 'He praised her so much, when you were out, that it was quite improper.' When told that the whole district knows of it, Fiodor Orlovsky reacts angrily: 'I'll go and stuff your district's mouth with this mustard pot.' The violence and the assertiveness are softened in the final version: Fiodor Orlovsky defends Elena's honour after his own appalling fashion, 'Nonsense. Nobody is her lover yet, but I soon shall be....'

It is odd (but typical of the mature Chekhov) that such a key dramatic element – the rumour of Voinitsky's and Elena's liaison that is to lead to the former's suicide, and then to general repentance – should be muted into the background. Any semblance of dramatic action has to wait for the arrival of the Serebriakovs to be announced, when Scene 6 brings in the professor, his daughter, his wife and his mother-in-law by his first wife. Then a critical mass of characters has been reached: ten actors on stage, negotiating tables set for tea, can hardly fail to explode. Yet Diadin's florid pleasantries dampen the powder: even Voinitsky teasing Sonia to anger cannot get the scene moving. Scene 6, too, is much cut: the version submitted to the censor gave far more rein to the senior males. Now Orlovsky senior loses much of his sententious self-praise and Serebriakov is deprived of a professorial anecdote. Even in this reduced form, however, the lunch scene is too heavy to be animated by Sonia's final outburst of anger when teased by Voinitsky.

As if only a demonic outsider could catalyse the assembly into action, Chekhov adds his eleventh character, the title role, in Scene 8, when Khrushchev, the Wood Demon burst in. But this is one of the few dynamic episodes in the Act. The rest seems a series of tableaux – as the Wood Demon is made to say when he appears: 'Why aren't I an artist? What a wonderful group!', which points to the static nature of the action so far. Now Fiodor Orlovsky is inspired to declare his love for an unnamed married woman and the audience has at least a mystery to grapple with; the spirit of contradiction comes alive and Voinitsky argues with the Wood Demon about the need to conserve trees. These, apart from Diadin's tragicomic account of his marriage, are the first speeches of the play to be lifted wholesale into *Uncle Vania* and it is instructive to see how what is a simple argument in *The Wood Demon* is developed into a three-sided discussion, with the intervention of Sonia, in *Uncle Vania*. This long and crowded scene – it amounts to over a third of the Act – ends with a final detonation: Voinitsky's anger explodes against his mother and then Serebriakov. Again Chekhov takes these dynamic moments to refine and reincorporate into *Uncle Vania*. Here, however, all the dramatic conflict peters out into gratitude for the meal and proposals for more delights, croquet with Fiodor, dinner with Iulia and fishing with the Wood Demon. At last the stage empties, or at least most of the cast retreats to the background to play croquet, and the act ends, as it began, with a dialogue, Voinitsky making an incompetent pass at Elena. The absurdly irritating Voinitsky and the lazily manipulative Elena are brilliantly evoked: Chekhov showed self-critical judgement when he also saved this scene for *Uncle Vania*. Nevertheless, like the preceding two scenes it had to be extensively reworked from the censor's version: Chekhov added the hawk which Fiodor Orlovsky toasts. Above all he reapportioned the speeches exhorting conservation. Originally the entire propaganda came from the Wood Demon's mouth: now Chekhov subtly dramatises the message by putting some of the speech into Voinitsky's mouth and letting the antagonist, Voinitsky, mimic the protagonist, the Wood Demon.

With hindsight from the vantage point of *Uncle Vania*, of course, it is easy to determine the failings and successes of this Act. The build-up of interest before the more flamboyant characters enter is a traditional device, but it would be a clever producer and a clever audience that would grasp the relations in this crowded terrace, where everyone appears to be preoccupied with a long-delayed lunch. When the *bête noire* Serebriakov finally enters, the effect is an anticlimax: he has little to say and that little is too banal to have any comic effect. Only towards the end of Scene 7 does conflict suddenly flare up and a brief bout of abuse from Voinitsky drives the professor away. He and the desperate younger Orlovsky, Fiodor, are the only dynamic characters, but their passion is not enough to shift the dialogue from the contemplative style of a novel and give it the force for interaction that we require from drama. Fiodor Orlovsky's Byronic pursuit of an unnamed married woman (whom we can guess to be Elena) seems in this idyllic setting to be mere hot air, while the Wood Demon's defence of the forests against the cynicism of Voinitsky and scepticism of Serebriakov sounds like a tract.

It is the end of Act 1 where we recognise the Chekhovian genius: Voinitsky's ill-concealed irritation results in an infantile outburst against the unholy alliance of his mother and the professor. Here we have one of the many parodies of Hamlet which form the core of Chekhovian comedy. Vania is a ridiculously superannuated Hamlet, his mother a desiccated Gertrude, Serebriakov a most ineffectual Claudius, and Elena a sophisticated Ophelia (note the water-imagery associated with her, as with Ophelia). The pathos of a man in his forties lapsing into Oedipal tantrums is at least shocking and funny enough to drive both the professor and the Wood Demon offstage. The last scenes, the eighth and ninth of the Act, are also typical of Chekhovian comedy and pathos, the anti-love scene in which Voinitsky makes all the wrong moves in his pursuit of Elena: the pathos is once again unmistakable, but the context so ridiculous that the comedy becomes cruel. Thus it is no wonder that these two final episodes of Act 1 were transferred almost intact into *Uncle Vania*.

We can thus fault Act 1 on its untidy characterisation and plotting. The potential of Orlovsky senior and both Zheltukhins for the plot is unrealised;

Orlovsky junior merely duplicates Voinitsky in his pursuit of Elena. The disparities between the professor as Voinitsky evokes him (a parasite), as he appears (sick and disorientated) and as he must have been (inspired and determined) to account for his success, is unaccounted for. Nevertheless there are a few strokes of genius: when Iulia constantly worries about her turkey chicks and Fiodor Orlovsky suddenly drinks to a passing hawk, the summery outdoor mood is darkened by imagery of prey and predator; the didactic impact of the Wood Demon's ecological speech is made subtler because it is narrated to us with mocking irony by Voinitsky.

Act 2 is another matter, a piece of confident, sustained genius. Chekhov must have realised this, for he transferred the whole act virtually intact into *Uncle Vania*, making only the most minimal changes. The author must have been satisfied with it: the censor's version and the lithograph are identical. The opening setting, in the middle of the night, with a hypochondriac professor in fear of imminent death, forcing the womenfolk to share his torment, comes straight from chapter five of the story he had been working on at the same time, *A Dreary Story*. Now, however, the colouring is different, for the professor is not the narrator, but a ridiculous figure wrapped up in a rug, yet another example of Chekhov's infantile manipulative antiheroes. The unwanted food on the sideboard makes for a far more effective prop than the lunch for which everyone has assembled in Act 1. The unseen outside world, with the ominous noise of the guard striking his wooden board and the window banging in the wind, operates on the audience with a mix of the comic and horrific. Here we no longer have the crowded party, with the audience as a confused stranger, but a series of one-to-one dialogues, those 'clarifications of relationships' (*vyiasnenie otnoshenii*, the Russian euphemism for rows), which are so enthralling and dramatically infectious. Act 2 of *The Wood Demon* is a new structure for Chekhov, and its succession of rows is to be the model for *The Seagull* and in *The Cherry Orchard* (notably Act 3). The technique is basically vaudeville – a central character on stage interacts with a series of new characters. In Scenes 1 to 4 the professor alienates in rapid succession, by the same egocentric pathos, his wife, his daughter, and his brother-in-law, before someone – the Wood Demon – takes pity and removes him. Then from Scenes 5 to 8 another succession of rows has Voinitsky at its centre, as he is rejected or reproached first by his beloved Elena (and in a monologue by himself), his friend and mentor the Wood Demon, his rival in love Fiodor and his sister Sonia. The third part of the Act, Scenes 8 to 10, focuses on Sonia as she reduces Voinitsky to tears and sends him offstage and then appeals for help and affection, first from the Wood Demon and then from Elena. The Act thus has a delightful symmetry: it divides into three parts, each involving three episodes with a new character, as it switches its focus from Serebriakov to Voinitsky and to Sonia, showing the chain of unhappiness and frustration with a callous cruelty that reduces into almost kindly pathos. When we study *Uncle Vania*, we shall see how even this taut economy could be improved on. But Act 2 is *The Wood Demon* at its greatest and an anticipation of Chekhov the dramatist of the 1890s.

Scene 1 is on the surface an argument (which Elena eventually wins) about whether the window should be open or closed, in the course of which the rift in the relationship is explored blow by blow. The banging window is one of Chekhov's first uses in drama of a device already established in his narrative prose, the intrusive noise that counterpoints a discussion. In his appeal for sympathy and his battle to reduce his unfeeling wife to tears, Serebriakov tries tack after tack – his morbid symptoms, his greatness (he may have the same disease as Turgenev), his academic needs (the urgent search for Batiushkov's poems), his age, his hard life, his retirement. It must be noted how much more pitiable Serebriakov is here than in *Uncle Vania*: here Chekhov lets Serebriakov lament that he worked too hard in Heidelberg and Paris to see either city. Nevertheless, Chekhov's technique is fundamentally comic, for Scenes 2 and 3 repeat the pattern of Scene 1: in Scene 2 Serebriakov fights the same battle with his daughter as with his wife, and in Scene 3 is at loggerheads with his brother-in-law, Voinitsky. Only in Scene 4 is the pattern broken and the Wood Demon succeeds in leading him off the stage to bed. Scene 5 not only begins the second part of the Act, but links up with the end of Act 1, as Voinitsky attempts to seduce Elena and allows us to judge how untrue are the rumours that he is already her lover. Chekhov was to re-use Voinitsky's flamboyant image for his feelings 'like a ray of light that has fallen into a pit' not just in *Uncle Vania*, but also in *The Duel* of 1891, where the similarly feckless Laevsky talks of being like a 'condemned man plunged into a deep well'.

With this renewed declaration of love, the plot (and the course of this false rumour is the nearest *The Wood Demon* has to a plot) finally begins to thicken: in Scene 6 the Wood Demon re-enters and catches Elena alone with Voinitsky. Then, however, the action stalls, and the end of that scene is the monologue that Chekhov is to develop so finely in *Uncle Vania*. Apart from its backward-looking lament, Voinitsky's monologue is remarkable for its introduction of a motif from Pushkin's and Tchaikovsky's *Eugene Onegin*. When he reflects about his missed opportunity to fall in love with Elena ten years ago, by saying 'That was so possible!' he echoes Tatiana's final reply to Onegin (who had missed the opportunity of responding to her love years before, when she was unmarried and in love): 'But happiness was so possible.' By introducing *Eugene Onegin* here with its motifs of violent death and unrequited love, tragedy enters by allusion.

In the last third of the Act, from Scene 9, Chekhov then develops his secondary theme, the love that Sonia feels for the Wood Demon, not so much unrequited as unnoticed. The breakdown in communication between them, however typical of Chekhov's couples in his prose, is too clumsily managed for the stage, however, and Sonia's final tears and monologue fit ill with her careful manipulation of the Wood Demon in the beginning of this section. Only when the Act and the plot were revised for *Uncle Vania* did Chekhov make this sad failure into a wry black comedy. Nevertheless, the last scene of the Act is psychologically cogent: Sonia and Elena, the two rival heroines, stalk each other, make peace and then (with innumerable pauses) conduct a conversation at cross-purposes, each talking of the Wood Demon, but pursuing their own aims. The act ends with the brilliant touch of the piano we expect to hear but which Serebriakov forbids to be played.

Act 3 moves from an abandoned dining-room to a crowded drawing-room. In *The Wood Demon* the Acts are linked by music (while in *Uncle Vania* they are linked by non-music, by a silent instrument). The piano music that Sonia and Elena were forbidden by the insomniac professor is heard at curtain rise, for Elena is playing Tchaikovsky, Lensky's aria from *Eugene Onegin*, an ominous touch, for this is what the jealous Lensky sings before he is killed in the duel with the merciless Onegin. (The presence of Tchaikovsky in *The Wood Demon* may have something to do with a visit that Tchaikovsky made to Chekhov in autumn 1889, when he proposed that they should collaborate on an opera based on Lermontov's *Bela*.) Voinitsky's comment that Lensky's aria is his favourite piece adds to the irony, for he is to be cast as the Lensky of the play, to die while his rival, the rake Fiodor Orlovsky, survives. But we are to be forced to wait until the end of the Act before the fatal shot rings out. The first half of Act 3 is almost unbearably disjointed and aimless: characters fill the stage until it is as crowded and unmanageable as in Act 1. Both Orlovskys and Voinitsky listen to Elena playing, to be joined by Sonia in Scene 2: all we learn from their interchanges is that two weeks have passed since Act 2 and that Sonia's pride has weakened enough to send for the Wood Demon. Elena makes a brief entry for Scene 3, while in Scene 4 the Zheltukhins enter and Voinitsky and Orlovsky leave.

The confused comings and goings, with no development, carry on for Scenes 6, 7 and 8. Some fifteen minutes' action amounts to no more than background to vaguely expected action: it is little wonder that the first half of Act 3 had to be changed out of all recognition when *Uncle Vania* was created. Only when Serebriakov enters in Scene 9 and prepares his bomb-shell, does the Act take off. The bombshell is typically Chekhovian: a character declares that he is impractical and helpless and then announces a ruthless plan for misappropriation worthy of a professional confidence trickster. Voinitsky's protest boils into hysteria in Scene 10 and Diadin vainly tries to pour oil on troubled waters in Scene 11: the action convincingly moves from a family argument to a Dostoevskian breakdown of all barriers and inhibitions. Scene 12 brings the Wood Demon (as announced in Scene 2). He has come not in response to the lovelorn Sonia but to save the forests from being sold by Serebriakov and surrendered to the axe. As in Act 2, the Wood Demon succeeds in driving Serebriakov offstage, but this time by infuriating him, not comforting him.

In the lull before the disaster Chekhov abandons Serebriakov's intrigue, the main plot he has built up in this Act (the third plot of the play), and returns to his original plots: the short Scenes 13 and 14 show the Wood Demon quarrelling first with Sonia and then with Elena (because he believes that she is Voinitsky's mistress). Scenes 15 and 16 finally produce violent action: Voinitsky shoots himself offstage and the curtain falls on hysteria. The second half of the Act, from Serebriakov assembling his audience to the gunshot, is fundamentally sound drama and, despite the radical alteration to the plot, it survives structurally intact in *Uncle Vania*. Nevertheless, it caused Chekhov some doubts, for the earlier version submitted to the censor is rather more melodramatic than the lithograph of 1890: the Wood Demon is much more intemperate with Serebriakov in Scene 12 and recruits Elena's support, while the Act closes not just with hysteria but with Fiodor Orlovsky's loud laughter 'imitating an operatic Mephistopheles'. The operatic influence that began the act with Tchaikovsky's *Eugene Onegin* is thus reinforced.

If any Act of *The Wood Demon* would dismay an audience, it is Act 4. Several of Chekhov's fourth Acts are problematical: as in *Uncle Vania* and *The Cherry Orchard*, so here the disaster that strikes in Act 3 leaves a sense of anticlimax. Chekhov solved the problem by making his fourth acts shorter, comically embarrassed aftermaths to catastrophe. But in *The Wood Demon* Act 4 is longer than any other Act; it also seems to belong to another play. The setting is at the water mill which Diadin leases from the Wood Demon: here he has been sheltering Elena who has fled her husband and his unhappy family. If Act 1 was built around lunch, Act 4 centres on a picnic tea. The entries and exits are extraordinarily clumsy, as in the first half of Act 3: Scene 1 has Elena and Diadin expounding the situation, again telling us that two weeks have passed since the previous act. The stage then empties (to Diadin's irritatingly static recurrent remark 'It's delightful!') while Scene 2 brings in new characters. In Scene 5 the plot is very crudely resolved, using the time-dishonoured device of a written message: the Wood Demon has read Voinitsky's diaries and everyone now realises that they had unjustly slandered Voinitsky and contributed to his death. The cliché of the missing diary that resolves the plot is as tired as the letter in Act 3 that Sonia finds and believes to incriminate Elena.

But, unbelievably, all the tragic responsibility revealed by the diary the Wood Demon has found is cast off and the subject is barely mentioned again. A happy end is in store. Scene by scene the stage fills up, as Iulia Zheltukhina, the Wood Demon, Semion, various workmen, Sonia and Zheltukhin and finally (by Scenes 7 and 8) Serebriakov, Orlovsky and his son Fiodor arrive for tea. In Scene 9 Elena makes her jack-in-the-box reappearance to confound them all and we have a stage with eleven speaking parts gathered like flies round the dog-cherry jam. It was not until the name-day party in Act 1 of *Three Sisters* that Chekhov showed himself capable of handling mass scenes, of maintaining the thread of dialogue and keeping up the choreography of a party. Act 4 of *The Wood Demon* is an object lesson in how not to stage a crowd scene.

Nevertheless, the purpose of the Act, to reverse all the alienation of the previous acts with a series of conciliations (however unlikely) now begins. Even the roué, Fiodor Orlovsky, urges marital conciliation, as unlikely as Don Giovanni urging the Commendatore to resume conjugal life with Donna Anna. At the end of Scene 9, Elena goes off with her husband, with yet another operatic flourish as she addresses him: 'Take me, Statue of the Commendatore, and perish with me in your twenty-six sad rooms', in a parody of Dargomyzhsky's version of *Don Giovanni*, the opera *The Stone Guest*. The hellishness is rather absurdly laid bare now by the appearance of a fire on the horizon (a technique Chekhov is to use far more effectively in *Three Sisters*) and the Wood Demon rushes off to save the burning forests, the external symbols of the souls of the characters that are being devastated by their quarrels. This equation of human nature and the planet is preceded by another more subtle piece of symbolism, the predatory bird.[5] In Act 1 Fiodor Orlovsky drank the health of a predatory hawk – presumably himself; he now tells Serebriakov an anecdote about the barn owl he failed to kill with nine shots from his wild-fowling gun – presumably a cryptic way of telling Serebriakov that Fiodor has failed to cuckold him.

The Zheltukhins and Fiodor Orlovsky also leave: the stage empties enough for dialogue to begin. In Scene 11 the Wood Demon embraces Sonia (to Diadin's expression of delight); in Scene 12 Fiodor proposes to Iulia. No fewer than three couples have been joined (or rejoined) in love: whether Chekhov was parodying or merely stretching to its limits the traditional happy ending of comedy, we cannot tell. But the incompatibility of this comedy with the catastrophe that ended the previous act is unbearable. Diadin's final words, 'It's delightful' deprive the audience of their right to their own reaction: it is beyond the ingenuity of any director to produce a performance where the spectator can leave the theatre without irritation.

Act 4 was, in fact, completely rewritten after the play was submitted to the censor: the first version is even worse, although it attempts to follow more closely upon the events of Act 3. Elena does not appear in Scene 1, and Scene 3 is taken up with the Wood Demon and Iulia repenting far more copiously their gullibility in believing the rumours of Voinitsky's involvement with Elena. The switch from repentance to merriment is made much more unapologetically than in the final version of *The Wood Demon*:

Zheltukhin recites one of Nekrasov's most original and cryptically lyrical poems *The Green Rustling* (*Zelionyi shum*) to justify this surrender to the joys of nature:

> The Noise of the Greenery comes roaring,/The Noise of the
> Greenery, the noise of spring!/The cherry orchards/Stand as
> if covered in milk,/They rustle quietly;/Warmed by the warm
> sun,/The mirthful pine/Trees rustle;.../And I keep hearing
> this song:/Love while you can,/Endure, while you can,/
> Forgive, while you can,/And God be your judge.

Why Chekhov abandoned this almost Bacchic reason for forgetting the death of Voinitsky, we cannot tell: in the final version Zheltukhin recites a much more civic and banal piece of Nekrasov, the exhortation: 'Sow the rational, good, eternal,/Sow! Thanks to you will be cordially said/By the Russian people.' The only reason for switching from mourning to celebration would be mystic, but Chekhov has erased it and substituted an irrelevant platitude.

The original version of Act 4 has Elena appearing in the final scene, as in the opening of Act 3, heralded by her playing Lensky's aria on the piano. This version of Act 4 is little more than half the length of the final version and, for all its weaknesses, it is far stronger than the revised version: the stage is not so crowded and the mysticism of Nekrasov's poem sets the atmosphere for a totally irrational change of mood from hysteria to happiness. Generally, Chekhov's revisions are severe reductions, cosmetic surgery of a high order. This is virtually the only occasion in which he padded and weakened his structure, a failure of creative instinct which we shall examine in the following chapter.

The Wood Demon's Reception and Literary Context

Few new-born infants have met with such rejection as *The Wood Demon*. Chekhov's own euphoria at having finally completed it by Svobodin's deadline in October 1889 was short-lived. He himself sensed that 'it has an unbearable construction' (Suvorin, 1 xi 89) and would need rewriting. The theatre censorship made a few cuts – references to God or the radical philosopher Lassalle. The 'Theatrical-Literary Committee of the Aleksandrinsky Theatre', however, controlled all access to state theatres: they met unofficially on 9 October 1889 and Svobodin read the play aloud to a committee which included some of Chekhov's sympathisers, notably the veteran Grigorovich. The committee was deeply unhappy with the play, not least because a university professor was cast as a villain – Russia was a country where a professor enjoyed the rank and respect due to an army general (within living memory a student had been flogged to death for assaulting a Moscow university professor). The committee members were worried about staging any play that the Grand Dukes (including the heir to the throne) might dislike on their forthcoming visit to the theatre, and unanimously told Svobodin that *The Wood Demon* was unfit for a benefit performance. Svobodin (letter to Lavrov, *Voprosy lit.* [1960] 1, 104), the midwife, was now lukewarm: '*The Wood Demon* which I longed to put on for my benefit *is no use* for stage performance in the view of the improvised committee, because it has none of the worn-out situations and characters, the stupid mediocre vulgarities now flooding the Aleksandrinsky theatre. It is boring, drawn-out, strange, like anything talented and profound in the eyes of people who understand nothing. I'll say too, as I did in Moscow, that *The Wood Demon* is no comedy in form, but the living characters, living speeches and temperaments are such that all the Aleksandrinsky rubbish is not worth half of the Chekhov play. Its unstageability [...] stands out as one of its defects.'

When Chekhov gave the play to Lensky, the actor-manager of the Maly theatre, the response was brutally frank (1/2 xi 89): 'I'll say one thing: write long stories. Your attitude to the stage and to dramatic form is too contemptuous, you respect them too little to write a drama. This form is more difficult

26

than narrative form, but you, forgive me, have been too spoiled by success to study dramatic form properly, starting with the alphabet, or to come to love it.' Nemirovich-Danchenko (who was not yet an associate of Stanislavsky, but was an experienced playwright and actor) also disliked the play: 'the author's stage sense seemed in some ways unfortunate. A play with no plot cannot succeed, but the major defect is its lack of clarity, when the audience cannot possibly grasp the core of the plot.' From a letter to Svobodin (11 xi 89) we can guess Suvorin's reaction too: 'I think it's a talented piece, very true to life, original, but not written to generally accepted formulas. I'll even say that Chekhov has ignored the "rules" too much, rules to which both actors and the public are used. I disliked just the end of Act 3 – Evgenia [*sic*, for Elena] could have simply run away to the mill – and the whole of Act 4, which should have been constructed differently. I would have thrown out two characters – both Orlovskys and other characters could then have been developed, especially that of the Wood Demon.'

Svobodin was franker to Suvorin than to Chekhov (Voprosy lit. [1960] 1, 104): 'You and I are completely at one: the comedy has two unnecessary characters, Elena's awkward flight to the mill with one of them and hence a natural remaking of all of Act 4, anyway not a versified ending of the play which is harmful for the action. But I told Anton Pavlovich all this, but he was as obstinate as the Petersburg climate. Did you notice the page and a half of verses crossed out in Act 4? He yielded on that to me at 4 a.m. after a three-hour argument, when I went to Moscow to fetch the play.'

Finally a fourth theatre, Abramova's Moscow theatre (by then an actors' co-operative) accepted the play: the chief actor Solovtsov wrote, 'Give us your Wood Demon and thus lead us who have got lost out of the woods onto the main road and do a good deed to the whole co-operative. Whatever terms you like.' Chekhov had revised the first three acts by 20 December; the fourth act was ready on Christmas day and the play opened on the 27th.[6] Some of these revisions we know of only by rumour – they do not appear in the lithograph version, and a few were actually to be used in *Uncle Vania*. Already the process of transmutation had begun. A few cuts and alterations can be found in the prompter's copy that has survived Abramova's production: some of these alterations, too, found their way into *Uncle Vania*.

Chekhov did not enjoy the production: after the Christmas Day rehearsal he wrote to Pleshcheev (27 xii 89) 'I didn't like the men on the whole and I haven't seen the women properly. [...] the play will be a great success in the provinces, for there is enough comic element and the people are all alive and familiar to the provinces.' To Suvorin (27 xii 89) he wrote, 'Act 4 is quite new. It owes its existence to you and Vladimir Nemirovich-Danchenko who read the play and gave me a few very practical bits of advice. The men don't know their parts and act quite well; the ladies know their lines and act badly [...]'. The reviewer Filippov wrote privately to Suvorin after the first performance: 'there were noisy curtain calls for the author and actors after the first three acts [...] light protests at the fourth which is weaker than the others [...] The audience could hear hardly anything of what the characters were saying.' Other reminiscences agree. Furthermore, actors from Korsh's theatre (into whose territory Abramova had muscled) had come to hiss and howl down the performance. The next four performances had diminishing returns: the last brought only 300 roubles, and by mid-January 1890 the play was taken off.

How Chekhov reacted to this fiasco, we do not know, but his letter to Suvorin, ostensibly about Bourget and Tolstoy, on the day of the première (27 xii 89) may be read as an attempt to justify and explain his intentions in writing a play with such an up-beat, life-enhancing ending. Dismissing Bourget's happy endings as falsifications, Chekhov attacks pessimists for corrupting the public: 'In Russia they help the devil to multiply the slugs and other slimy creatures we call intellectuals. [...] an intelligentsia which is unpatriotic, depressed, colourless, which gets drunk on one glass and visits 50-kopeck brothels [...]'

The reviewers were scathing: S.V. Fliorov (under the name of Vasiliev) condemned it in the phrases that critics had often used against Chekhov's prose:

> ...boring...the spectator is right and the author at fault...it tells us a story...the characters are all on the same plane...the play has no real comic centre.... Art consists not of simple reproduction of real life. If so, there would be no need for art. Photography would replace painting, affidavits and police statements would replace literature. Chekhov pretends that he doesn't know how important time is and spends time on endless conversation. Do you know how Act 1 passes? It is spent on a birthday lunch served in the garden. [...] Every new arrival first eats then sits down to lunch [...] In Act 4 all the characters again gather. Just as in Act 1 the table is laid, the food they have brought is set out and they set to. [...] The Wood Demon is never the central figure of this play. He is just an accessory, like all the other characters. [...] the action is limited by eating: they are always sitting down to table and then having conversations [...] all they do is talk, saying anything that comes into their heads.... No authorial synthesis...no conclusion...no personal thought or personal artistic feeling. (*Moskovskie vedomosti* [1890] 1 i 90)

Reviewers working for journals where Chekhov had been a collaborator were more gentle and conscientious in their reactions. 'Niks' [N.P. Kicheev], a contributor to 'The Alarm Clock', felt that the play aimed higher than *Ivanov* in attacking a social disease: 'the urge to destroy irresponsible egotism, a complete inability to be altruistic...this is the morbid vein in contemporary society to which Mr Chekhov's new play is dedicated.' But he felt the flaws were fatal: 'Many pointless episodes (for example Diadin's appearance in Act 3) [...] the obvious monotony of the devices (lunch in Act 1, supper in Act 2, tea in Act 4). [...] I see only *scenes* that suffer from being too protracted and have too little action, but are indubitably written freshly and with talent. I'll say more: *there is no play* – because of the clumsily constructed scenes we see a *tale* or even a novel, *unfortunately*, squeezed into dramatic form.' (*Novosti dnia* [1890] 1 i 90).

The critic of *Novoe vremia* was not just unimpressed, he had failed to grasp much of the plot: 'The spectator seems to be reading an interesting, cleverly written story or a novel, which for no earthly reason has been poured into dramatic form. Apparently the laws of the stage are ignored by the author; as a play *The Wood Demon* is long and limp; the young writer's work has exceptional merits which alternate with faults that are a consequence of turning a novel into a comedy [...] the Wood Demon and his love intrigue with a girl who is an intellectual landowner are not the main interest in the comedy, while the marital misfortunes of a sick old professor and his young wife or the love of an elderly man for the professor's wife, the intrigues of a Don Juan with a young housewife are not worked out properly.'

These were fair comments. Other attacks were grotesque, particularly that of Ivanov in *Artist*, a journal to which both Svobodin and Chekhov contributed: he accused Chekhov of taking pleasure in denigrating elderly professors and could not see why Voinitsky could possibly regret his long years of service to Serebriakov. Some of Ivanov's points were more pertinent in that they show a Russian conservative's resistance to Chekhovian innovations: 'Everyone is fed up with banal conversations while drinking and eating either at home or with friends, and if you want to hear ten times people enquiring about others' health or quarrelling with each other then there's no need at all to go to the theatre and endure four acts of a "comedy". Chekhov's talent is undoubtedly higher than the play he has written and its peculiarities can probably be explained by hasty work or a sad error about the most essential properties of any dramatic work.'[7] Father-figures such as the revered prose-writer Grigorovich were puzzled by *The Wood Demon* as a lapse: Grigorovich, sensing the play's novelistic structure around mounting social scandals, exclaimed, 'This is something half-way between *The Devils* and *The Brothers Karamazov*.'[8]

After this hostile reaction Chekhov fled to Petersburg and hastily completed the arrangements for his suicidal, self-sacrificial journey to the penal island of Sakhalin. The play was unlucky and he refused all requests to publish it, demanding that *Artist* return the copy he had sent them. The chief supporters of the play were just as ill-starred: by 1892 both Svobodin and Abramova had died. The play remained an unhappy memory. In 1899 Urusov made a last plea: 'Since January a new magazine, "Pantheon", devoted to the theatre, has been published, edited by Diagilev, who together with a group of young writers and artists ("The World of Art") confesses a cult of Chekhov more than anyone else. I advised them to ask you to let them have *The Wood Demon* for printing, as a remarkable variant of *Uncle Vania*.... They grabbed at the idea with delight.' Chekhov refused Urusov (and Diagilev) for the last time: 'I cannot print *The Wood Demon*. I hate this play and I am trying to forget about it. Whether it is the play's fault or the circumstances in which it was written and staged, I don't know, but it would be a real blow to me if any forces retrieved it from under the barrel and brought it back to life. There you have a shining example of perverted parental feeling.'

This one supporter of the play persisted: A.I. Urusov (1843-1900), a lawyer and critic, who was to write the first article in the French press about Chekhov, pressed him for years to allow an amateur production of the play; for ten years he periodically begged Chekhov to let him publish it, and it is partly because of Urusov's importunacy that Chekhov took the manuscript and revised it into a new play, contrary to his ruthless practice of abandoning failures.

But before we examine the wreck and salvage of the play, perhaps we should make a case for what *The Wood Demon* attempted to achieve and what was not necessarily resurrected in *Uncle Vania*.

First of all, like *The Seagull*, but unlike *Uncle Vania*, *The Wood Demon* has a dangerously personal input. (In April 1901 Suvorin's irrepressible wife, Anna Ivanovna, was to write to Chekhov that she knew *Uncle Vania* by heart and roared with laughter whenever she saw it because she recognised all her family in the characters [Russian State Library archive 331 59 46].) It is not just Suvorin who is present in Orlovsky senior's complacent love for his aggressive son and in Serebriakov's *mésalliance* with Elena: the central implausibility of the play can be seen as a transfer of an extraordinary sequence of events in the Chekhov family. Two weeks after Voinitsky's suicide, the characters celebrate marriage. The autobiographical relevance is clear, if indirect. The play's setting recalls the estate where Chekhov spent summers of 1888 and 1889 on the river Psiol, near Sumy, an estate run by the Lintvariov family, intellectual landowners whose characters share some aspects of Sonia and Iulia. There in June 1889 Chekhov's brother Nikolai had died a harrowing death of typhoid and tuberculosis; the day before he died Anton (who acted as doctor as well as the effective head of the family), and his younger brother Ivan abandoned their brother and went off touring, while the eldest brother Alexander nursed the dying man. Nikolai with his impossible moods, his lies and psychotic behaviour had upset the family's life for a decade. His death was undoubtedly a relief, but the guilt of the survivors is obvious from the Chekhov family letters. Alexander, the eldest son, wrote to their father:

> Kolia died in my arms. Mama came very late and I had to wake Misha to tell him that Kolia had died. Everyone is howling. Anton is the only one not crying and that is bad.

Misha, the youngest, described the funeral to his father, emphasising food as does the play:

> ...all the ordinary people were given a pie, a kerchief and a glass of vodka each, while the clergy and the Lintvariovs had lunch and tea with us. After dinner mama and I went back to the cemetery, mama grieved and wept for a while and we went back. Be well, give our regards to aunt and come and see us. Your son, Mikhail Chekhov.

Pavel Egorovich's paternal letter to Anton was typical of his stereotyped responses, 'tramontane' in the vocabulary of the family:

> I have read your letter [...] it was very joyful for my parental heart that Kolia took Holy Communion and that his burial followed Christian rites. [...] Your aunt grieves very much, moaning and coughing, she hadn't known of Kolia's end and I hadn't told her.

Three weeks later, as if nothing had happened, Alexander announced that he had married Natalia Golden, his children's nurse, since his common-law wife Anna had died the previous year, his concubine and, most embarrassing, Anton's mistress only four years before: 'Dear Papa, I have kept my promise to you. Today at 12 p.m. I married Natalia Aleksandrovna. Mama and Misha blessed us. Father Mitrofan conducted the ceremony. After the wedding we visited Kolia's grave.' The glaring inconsistency of *The Wood Demon*, death in Act 3 and joyful unions in Act 4, thus reflects, as much as the idyllic Ukrainian setting, the incongruity of the tragedy and reconciliation in Chekhov's own family. *The Wood Demon* was an attempt to sketch and perhaps illuminate family conflicts about which we can only guess.

The second powerful current underlying the play is a mystical cult of nature's healing power, the Wood Demon and the miller Diadin representing living forests and moving water, reconciling quarrelling urban man. Much of this current was weakened by the changes that Svobodin insisted on:

Nekrasov's poem *The Green Rustling* which was cut from the lithographed text is the hidden source of this current. The poem belongs to Scene 6 of Act 4, where it is recited by Zheltukhin to the Wood Demon, between Serebriakov's announcement that he has learnt his lesson so much from what has happened that he can write a whole treatise for posterity and Sonia shuddering at a sudden noise, that of peasants catching crayfish. Zheltukhin quotes only the second half of Nekrasov's poem, a poem familiar to all Russian audiences of the time: the narrator is a peasant whose wife admits that she has been unfaithful while he was away in the city. All winter, locked up in the hut, although he loves her, he prepares to kill her: only the approach of spring, the *green rustling* makes him lower his knife and able to forgive. The moral 'Love while you can, / Endure while you can, / Forgive while you can, / And God be your judge' is clearly relevant to Chekhov's last Act, while the benign influence of Diadin's mill after the labyrinth and vault-like Serebriakov house in which Acts 2 and 3 have taken their fatal course clearly corresponds to Nekrasov's blossoming trees which make the betrayed husband forget the blizzards of winter and forgive the erring wife.

The importance of nature in moulding the mood of the characters is important in all of Chekhov's plays, but in *The Wood Demon* it takes on the dominant force, almost displacing the central human protagonist, which it is to have in *The Seagull* (the lake) or *The Cherry Orchard* where the orchard's branches and blossom reach right into the house. The choice of a poem as a central text to which the whole play alludes is also a device of the mature Chekhov. If the initial central reference of *The Wood Demon* is Nekrasov's *The Green Rustling*, then *The Seagull* can be related to Hamlet or to Maupassant's prose read aloud in Act 2 (his travelogue *Sur l' eau*), and *The Cherry Orchard* clearly expands A.K. Tolstoy's poem *The Scarlet Woman* (or *The Sinner*) which is recited in Act 3. One cannot help thinking that Act 4 of *The Wood Demon* would have been less of a disaster if Chekhov had not given way to Svobodin's insistence on cutting the core reference to Nekrasov's *The Green Rustling*.

On a rational plane the cult of nature in *The Wood Demon* surprises us no longer: but for its time it was original, and Chekhov raised his message from the laments of simple countrymen in his stories and made it the arguments of educated men in his plays. In *Panpipes* the hero complains, 'They are cutting the forests, and they are burning and drying up and nothing new grows. Whatever does grow is cut down straight away; it sprouts today and tomorrow before you can blink people have felled it, so it is everywhere until nothing is left.' This is lifted into the Wood Demon's plea to Serebriakov, thus making the first ecological drama in literature: 'Don't do it…. To fell a thousand trees, to destroy them for the sake of two or three thousand roubles…so that posterity will curse our barbarity!' The play takes up themes that were becoming popular in Russia's agricultural and horticultural journals, the threat of deforestation and its connection with degeneration in human life. The message of *The Wood Demon*, however clumsy, is that the destruction of the environment and of people's lives by selfishness are closely linked processes. We shall see how in *Uncle Vania* Chekhov makes his message sharper, partly because these processes of destruction have worsened but also because his dramatic technique is subtler.

The Wood Demon himself was originally meant to be a spirit rather than a mere human being, and in his revisions Chekhov removed many of the references to him (as a satyr or a Mephistopheles, for instance) and the more emotional of his outbursts, reducing him to a more ordinary level. If a cult of nature is one of the mainsprings of the play, then a Pan-like God, the Wood Demon, might be expected to take on folkloric, supernatural overtones. In fact, Russian folklore plays a very small role in Chekhov's work: in *The Wood Demon*, with a forest spirit and a water spirit (Diadin) Chekhov uses more folk motifs than anywhere else. True, in 1884 he had written a story, *The Naïve Wood Demon*, but elves, sprites and spirits are outside his usual range. In *The Wood Demon* the folklore elements are used in a way that faintly recalls the *style moderne* to which Chekhov's literary devices have been compared: the horror and supernatural have given way to a balletic interplay of images, emphasising more the sexuality of the water-nymph and the wood-demon as they interact with the merely human.

The supernatural element implied by presence of a forest and a water-god is reinforced by mythological imagery which contrasts the life of nature with the deadliness of the interior scenes: the Serebriakov-Voinitsky house is described by the professor in Act 2 as a 'vault', in Act 3 as a 'labyrinth'. Elena, when she agrees to return to him, tells him in Act 4, rephrasing Dargomyzhsky's opera *The Stone Guest*, 'Then take me, Commendatore, back to your twenty-six rooms'. The hyperbolic house was always a feature of the Chekhovian play, but here the interior setting begins to take on the frightening hostility, the doom we sense in the house in *Three Sisters* or *The Cherry Orchard*.

The irrational element in Chekhov is reinforced by music: *The Wood Demon* like *Ivanov* uses serious music to make its point, referring to operas by Offenbach, Tchaikovsky, Dargomyzhsky and Rubinstein that all deal with a demonic hero (Menelaus, Eugene Onegin, Don Juan or the Commendatore, Lermontov's Demon) dealing out death to rivals and perdition to women). Thus the dangerous hero – Fiodor Orlovsky, Voinitsky or Serebriakov – is parodied and disarmed. Dargomyzhsky's *Rusalka* is also quoted by Zheltukhin in Act 4 to introduce the idea of magical, if dangerous, shores where lovers may reunite. In later plays Chekhov has a lighter touch: he uses not opera but operetta or vaudeville (Sidney Jones's *The Geisha* underlies *Three Sisters*). But here as elsewhere Chekhovian characters sing snatches of popular romances which ironically counterpoint the action.

The greatest innovation of *The Wood Demon* is what the critics most loathed: the accompaniment of eating and drinking to life's tragedies and joys. In the Chekhov family, constantly crowded with relatives, friends and customers, from boyhood almost to death, Chekhov's life was a sequence of table sittings. What strikes us now is not the realism but the incongruity, even the slight menace of life's dramas taking place at table. Act 1, Scene 3, when Voinitsky asks Diadin to cut him a slice of ham, makes irrelevance sinister as well as comic: Diadin declares, 'Beethoven or Shakespeare couldn't slice like this. Only the knife is blunt.' (*Sharpens one knife against another.*) Zheltukhin, quivering, interjects: 'Stop it, Waffles, I can't stand it.' Chekhov's later uses of breaking saucers or half-eaten apples is neater, but *The Wood Demon* has set a precedent.

The sinister irrelevance is at its most famous in the breaking string of *The Cherry Orchard*. Nearly all Chekhov's plays have offstage noises apparently at odds with the drama: here, in Act 4, Sonia quivers at a noise whose nature Chekhov does not specify, only to be told that it is 'Peasants catching crayfish.' The hint at another life offstage shrinks the dimensions of the action and breaks the traditional closed framework. The reference to strongly emotive, even aromatic food, especially fish, is typically Chekhovian, once again deliberately destroying the unity of the imagery.

We have listed these innovations as a possible case for the defence of *The Wood Demon* as a play with a right to an autonomous existence. Possibly producers will find a way to convince the public, perhaps by staging it, as Artsybashev has staged Act 1 of *Three Sisters* in his Moscow Experimental Theatre, as a banquet to which the audience are invited to mingle, like Banquo's ghosts, with the cast. Certainly a successful handling of the three acts as three meals is the key to unlock the play's stage potential.

Until the 1960s, when a desperate thirst for new Chekhov drove producers to innovate, *The Wood Demon* remained unperformed in the West, even though it had been translated by Koteliansky into English as early as 1926. In Russia one might have thought that the social optimism of *The Wood Demon*, with a protagonist who declares that 'real heroes to lead us out of the dark forest' are needed, that he 'can become a hero', would make the play and its hero seem a forerunner of Gorky and his hyperactive, prophetic idealists. However, only in 1960 did the Moscow Arts Theatre stage *The Wood Demon*, and well enough to persuade many spectators that the play had a right to an autonomous existence in the repertoire.

In 1993, Sergei Zhenovach, a director interested in peripheral genres, vaudeville and melodrama, singled out *The Wood Demon* as a musical play – almost an operetta. Zhenovach tried to make the play's naïvety and clumsiness positive primitive attributes with a happy end, relating it to the genre, rather than to Chekhov's canon. The final acts of mutual forgiveness give this production a Buddhist contemplative joy. While the Moscow critics were unhappy with such stylisation, at least Zhenovach had explored ways of making the play viable. Zhenovach's comments: [9]

> The only 'wide open' play is *The Wood Demon*. It has remained isolated. I think that if it had been supported, Chekhov's plays would have taken another path and not 'closed in'. But from the very first minute we guess that the cherry orchard will be sold, that the sisters will not go to Moscow [...] People are trapped in an impasse, preserved in aspic. One way or another, they perish. *The Wood Demon* is the only play that gives us a feeling of prospects. [...] It's not the point that the finale includes two marriages and the Serebriakov's reconciliation. Even here we can predict that Sonia and the Wood Demon's marital relationship will not be wholly good, that the conflict will continue, if at another level. Iulia and Fiodor Orlovsky are unlikely to be happy. Probably he will run wild and she will have lots of children, and Iulia will turn into something like Natasha. [...] *The Wood Demon* is not optimistic. (I don't think there are any good optimistic plays. But the finale is open, the situation is not exhausted, it has a continuation).

However, Zhenovach has failed to fill the theatre on the Malaia Bronnaia; despite a marvellous, airy polygonal set to accommodate the play's multiple couples and a brilliant performance by Sergei Batalov that raises Diadin to a mythological plane that matches that of the Wood Demon himself, the spectator can only concur that the play, and particularly Act 4, is simply bad theatre.

Abroad, neither in Germany nor in England, have productions convinced any spectators of the special merits of *The Wood Demon* vis-à-vis *Uncle Vania*. Curiously, in 1902, *The Wood Demon* was the first Chekhov play to be performed in Bulgaria.

Notes to Part One

1. This play is referred to as *Fatherlessness* by modern Russian critics; many (including me) believe that to be the title of an even earlier juvenile work which Chekhov wrote and destroyed.

2. A full account of this extraordinary man has, however, yet to be compiled, but his diaries (published in Germany in 1923 and republished in Russia [*Dnevnik*, Moscow: Novosti, 1992]) give a picture of his melancholy, free-thinking involvement in politics, theatre and friendships.

3. Boris and Nastia were the names of two of Suvorin's children: in Spring 1888 Suvorin seriously proposed that Chekhov should marry Nastia (then 10 years old) and thus become a co-owner of *New Times*.

4. Saveli Senderovich's article (see Bibliography) shows that Chekhov singled out the image, icon and name of St George and that Egor/Georgi was a name with resonance in the Chekhov family.

5. The symbolism of predatory birds, which began with the professor Blagosvetlov's 'order of the White Eagle' in Chekhov's outline for the play, links *The Wood Demon* with *A Dreary Story*. In the story owls shriek, while the professor sees himself as an eagle among chickens; in the play the professor is compared to an owl, the Wood Demon aspires to be an eagle, while Orlovsky is associated with a hawk (his name means 'eagle') and Elena (anticipating *The Seagull*) calls herself a caged canary.

6. Maria Moritsevna Abramova [Heinrich] (1865-92), a provincial actress, ran a private theatre for the 1889-90 season in Moscow. She offered a 'good price' for *The Wood Demon*.

7. Later the same I.I. Ivanov, on the Theatrical-Literary Committee of the Imperial Theatres, opposed the staging of *Uncle Vania*.

8. The critique that hit hardest, however, came from the poet Aleksei Pleshcheev. He wrote to the author (24 iv 1890) at length: '... *The Wood Demon* did not satisfy me and this is the first piece by you that [...] has left no impression on me [...] As for Voinitsky, strike me dead, I can't understand why he shot himself, [...]' (*Slovo, Sbornik vtoroi. K desiatiletiiu smerti A.P. Chekhova* [Moscow, 1914] pp. 279-81).

9. See 'Moskovskii nabliudatel'', *Teatral'nyi zhurnal* (1993) 11-12, pp. 28-33, for a review of the production and the director's comments.

Part Two

The Conversion into *Uncle Vania*

There is nothing unusual about Chekhov radically revising his earlier work. Very many of the stories of the mid-1880s were completely rewritten, some even retitled, when he republished them in his Collected Works in the 1900s; usually, the earlier version has disappeared, relegated to the footnotes of an academic edition. Of the earlier plays, *Ivanov*, too, underwent considerable transformation and the academic edition prints both versions, the tragedy of 1888 and the drama of 1889. But few of Chekhov's revisions transformed a text as the conversion of *The Wood Demon* into *Uncle Vania*.[1] Why he did it is not puzzling: innate thrift led him to recycle all his waste work.

Uncle Vania was first published in 1897. When the revision actually took place is not altogether clear. The various versions of *The Wood Demon* from the censorship text to the prompter's copy already show a process of cutting. The process was so continuous that Chekhov himself often drew no distinction between the two plays, referring to *Uncle Vania* as a play he had written in 1890, not 1897. We might presume that during the journey to Sakhalin that took up most of 1890 no more was done. But a letter from Pavel Svobodin to Chekhov implies that, while crossing Siberia, Chekhov might well fill time writing, or rewriting a play: 'Pogozhev has told me that for any prospective plays written on the journey to Sakhalin to be accepted and staged you have only to write me an ordinary letter [...] and say that you entrust me to hand such-and-such a play (leave a blank space for inserting the title) to the Committee...'. But on the eve of his departure Chekhov had handed over the text of *The Wood Demon* for lithography, which suggests that a revision was not what he had in mind.

The distinctive features of *Uncle Vania*, however, suggest that most of the radical rewriting was carried out not in 1890 but in autumn 1896, after the completion and before the disastrous first Petersburg performance (17 October 1896) of *The Seagull*: like *The Seagull*, *Uncle Vania* has no scene breaks. Until 1895, when Chekhov talked of 'a new play' he was writing, he clearly meant *The Seagull*. In November 1895 he once again refused to release a copy of *The Wood Demon* to the play's sole admirer, Urusov, on the grounds that the text would have to be retrieved and reread: presumably, he would have placated Urusov if he could, by announcing a new version of the play.

The last pieces of circumstantial evidence are to be found in the notebooks and diary entries Chekhov made in summer and autumn 1896, phrases which are incorporated into *Uncle Vania* but are absent from *The Wood Demon*. Thus Chekhov notes on 20 August 1896 the arrival of his guest, the editor Menshikov: 'In dry weather M. goes about in galoshes, with an umbrella, so as not to die of sunstroke...' and then has Uncle Vania remark of Serebriakov in Act 1: 'It's hot, stuffy, but our great scholar is wearing an overcoat, galoshes and has an umbrella and gloves.'[2] Both notebooks and diary carry a reflection which is given to Astrov in Act 4 of *Uncle Vania* (Notebooks II, 44): 'He used to think cranks were sick. But now he considers it normal for people to be cranks.'; (Notebooks I, 69): 'He used to think cranks were sick, but now he considers that it is the normal state for a human being to be a crank'.

The trauma of *The Seagull*'s reception in St Petersburg makes it unlikely that Chekhov immediately set to work on a new play. However, a letter to Suvorin (2 xii 96) announces the birth: 'I still have two big plays that are not typeset: *The Seagull* which you know, and *Uncle Vania*, which nobody in the world knows.' The text of *Uncle Vania* was submitted to Suvorin's printers a week later for inclusion in a book, *Plays*, and on 18 January 1897 the final proofs were returned: a nine-year evolutionary process was virtually over. Only minor changes were made when the play was included in Chekhov's collected works in 1901.

The most interesting question about the revision is not why (thrift) or when (autumn 1896), but how. A comparison of the new text with the old shows the butterfly emerging from its dramatic cocoon.

A Reading of *Uncle Vania*: Act 1

First of all, the cast of the play is ruthlessly cut: the Serebriakov-Voinitsky family remains, but both Zheltukhins, Leonid and Iulia, and both Orlovskys, Ivan and Fiodor, vanish. The Wood Demon's surname is changed from Khrushchev to Astrov – he is no longer a 'landowner who has qualified in medicine', but just a 'doctor'. Diadin is renamed Telegin, and is now demoted to 'an impoverished landowner'. The workforce is reduced to one workman. Only one character is added: the nurse, Marina. The nurse is of primary importance, however small her part: her faith is not only in utter contrast to the doubts that beset the main characters, but she acts as the only anchor for both Serebriakov and Astrov, the only provider of final answers to their distress.

The consequences of these cuts are manifold. For one thing, the remaining characters are isolated, friendless without their 'pair'. Serebriakov has no Orlovsky to confide in, Sonia is deprived of Iulia, Voinitsky has no Fiodor to compete with, the doctor/Wood Demon has no Zheltukhin for a foil. The disappearance of the confidante leads to the disappearance of confidence. Moreover, characters are not just removed from the scene, they are merged with the survivors. Fiodor Orlovsky is partly incorporated into Astrov, an integration of Mr Hyde with Dr Jekyll,[3] while the domesticated aspects of Iulia are spliced into Sonia's affectionate aspirations – many of their phrases are not cut, but reassigned. The grouping of characters changes fundamentally: they can be divided into firstly masters – the outsiders Serebriakov and Elena, in control of their destiny; secondly servants – Telegin, Marina, even Maria Vasilievna accepting their subjugation; thirdly three central figures – Astrov, Voinitsky and Sonia resisting their fate. Alternatively, a sparse symmetry, a new 'doubling' of characters, of an egotist with an altruist, arises, with Serebriakov and Telegin representing old age, Maria Vasilievna and Marina maternity, Elena and Sonia heroines in pursuit of love, Astrov and Voinitsky as heroic misfits.

The other consequence is to establish a unity of place: instead of three settings on three estates, now that the Zheltukhins have vanished and Diadin has been deprived of his mill, only the Serebriakov-Voinitsky house and garden remain. At the same time Chekhov has moved his action two hundred miles east, from the idyllic well-watered countryside of the north-east

Ukraine to a tired and over-populated central Russian landscape somewhere on the railway-line between Serpukhov and Kharkov; at the same time he has moved the play's setting from a Romantic's healing nature to a Symbolist's wasteland.

Act 1 opens at the same time (early afternoon) and in a garden, with tables laid for tea. But the expectations are gone: the guests are all present and all familiars. Nothing from Scenes 1 and 2 of *The Wood Demon* is used: instead Chekhov opens with a completely new scene and character. Marina offers Astrov tea and, guessing that he'd prefer vodka, introduces a completely new note of despondency and decay into the work. Firstly, vodka, secondly, the haunting presence of Serebriakov's first wife now dominate the action. The doctor's chief motif, completely absent from the early play, is distress at the conditions around him and guilt at himself – and medicine and society – being unable to cope with it. The repeated motif 'life is boring, stupid, dirty' (borrowed from Chekhov's letters to his brother Aleksandr) is utterly at odds with the expressions of delight and expectations that punctuate *The Wood Demon*. (To his Moscow Arts Theatre production Stanislavsky added hordes of mosquitoes, a device he also used in Act 2 of *The Cherry Orchard*, to torment Astrov and later Voinitsky.) Now the positive element is different and belongs entirely to Marina: to Astrov's desperate question, whether future generations will remember his sacrifice, Marina firmly replies 'People won't remember, but God will.' This is not only a new scene, but a new technique: from *The Seagull* on, Chekhov's main characters introduce themselves by enumerating their faults and misfortunes, a self-definition which the rest of the play only annotates. Astrov's disillusion, Voinitsky's decay and Elena's 'episodic' role are all announced by themselves.

Hereupon Voinitsky enters. In *The Wood Demon* his entry with Orlovsky is low key, with no guidance given to his expression or dress. Now Chekhov is specific and intriguing: 'He has had a sleep after breakfast and looks crumpled...he straightens his dandyish tie.' The incongruity of the crumpled sleepiness and fancy tie is typical of mature Chekhov: it forces the audience to solve a visual enigma. In Russia sleeping after a meal was no traditional siesta but the mark of a degenerate landowner, while the tie – a typical 'vestimentary marker', a garment that signals to the audience how they should interpret the character – suggests aspirations to, or vestiges of, past pride. These aspirations and their nature become only too clear once Voinitsky talks of his new sister-in-law Elena. Imitating Maupassant, who skilfully uses women's clothes to mark their moods, Chekhov had begun systematically to use 'vestimentary markers' in his plays from *The Seagull* onwards.

Voinitsky's first speech, punctuated by slapping at Stanislavsky's mosquitoes, echoes Astrov's in its confession of degeneration; while Astrov has fallen into a rut, Voinitsky has been thrown out of his routine by Serebriakov's arrival. Their brotherhood of opposites, as active and inactive failed males, is now much more subtly and forcefully implied. Now Chekhov inserts a new passage: Serebriakov and his court – Maria Vasilievna, Telegin and Sonia – pass across the background, an absurd picture heightened by Voinitsky's remark on this second set of 'vestimentary markers' (Serebriakov's overcoat, galoshes, umbrella and gloves). The negotiations that take place in *The Wood Demon* around the lunch table are omitted: Telegin, unlike Diadin, is not entrusted with a knife or ham; this is a much worse run household, in which only the samovar is left to unite the household around the table, and the samovar has been allowed to go off the boil – a reproach by implication to the women of the house, preoccupied as they are by the struggle for power. Of the table talk only a sample, a mere fraction, of Diadin's pompous florid speech is left: in *The Wood Demon* this is consistent with his constant expressions of delight; in *Uncle Vania*, however, his happiness is an absurd incongruence with the overall despondent mood.

The first large area of Act 1 of *The Wood Demon* to be transferred almost entirely is Scene 3, its most dynamic scene: Voinitsky's attack on the enigma of Serebriakov's success. Now his diatribe is no longer spurred on by Orlovsky's cynical prompts, but by an Astrov whose moral detachment from the miseries of the household seems, at first, cryptic. Only the operatic and literary elements are removed from Voinitsky's satirical denunciation: Serebriakov is no longer magnificent, 'as jealous as Othello', but absurd – he now 'strides like a demi-God.' Voinitsky's obsession is brought out even more by a dramatic counterpoint that never worked on the crowded stage of *The Wood Demon*: while Voinitsky praises Elena's beauty, Telegin is engaged in an absurd panegyric of the scene, praising the non-existent harmony and peace around the table, to Marina. This episode not only becomes absurd, it is also stripped of anything positive about the living: Voinitsky omits to praise Elena's piano-playing; there is no Zheltukhin to praise Sonia's voice. In *Uncle Vania* only the dead Vera Petrovna is praiseworthy, and she has no peers. Throughout *Uncle Vania* we see Chekhov operating a process of refinement, in which anything surplus to the necessary impact is removed: Telegin's absurd, endearing sententiousness and Astrov's sardonicism are all the sharper for being half the length of Diadin's and Orlovsky's responses. The effect is both more comic and more morbid. All that Stanislavsky left of the continuous feasting in *The Wood Demon* was to have Voinitsky reach for strawberries and cream once his outburst is over.

Uncle Vania then moves on by sharp contrast: the male trio is interrupted by the arrival of a female trio, Elena, Sonia and Maria Vasilievna, who each act autonomously – Elena is offhand first to Astrov, then to Telegin; Sonia makes a conspicuous contrast by affectionately offering dinner to Astrov and tea to Telegin; Maria Vasilievna buries herself in her pamphlets.

Chekhov has discarded Scenes 4 and 5 of *The Wood Demon* and, as he has now removed Serebriakov from the Act, keeps nothing from Scene 6 except for Telegin's remark about the cold pie (now cold tea). Now Telegin's introduction of himself is no longer a greeting to a visitor, but a bitterly ironic reminder of Elena's total alienation from her new household: 'You may have noticed that I dine every day with you.' The first half of Scene 7, with the arrival of the Wood Demon, has also been scrapped, since Astrov is on stage continuously until the Act has almost ended, and Fiodor Orlovsky no longer exists to pursue Elena. (Instead, Stanislavsky had Astrov silently pushing Elena on the swings.) All that survives of that scene from *The Wood Demon* is its most inspired touch, the hawk that flies overhead: its ghost hovers when Marina briefly reappears rounding up the speckled hen and her chicks (members of the cast that most directors, unlike Stanislavsky, omit), 'in case the crows get them.'

The second half of Scene 7 of *The Wood Demon* is, however, relatively dynamic, for now a row brews: this is an argument between the Wood Demon and Voinitsky on the need to conserve forests by burning peat, not wood. It is beautifully redistributed by Chekhov, a rearrangement he had already attempted when revising *The Wood Demon* for its lithograph version. First of all he rearranges the order of events: an argument flares up between Voinitsky and his mother in *The Wood Demon* after the Wood Demon has preached his sermon. In *Uncle Vania* this ludicrous row about Voinitsky's loss of his 'radiant personality' precedes Astrov's 'ecological' speech, so that it now takes place against a background of simmering tension. Sonia still silences her uncle (Chekhovian uncles, whether Shabelsky in *Ivanov*, Sorin in *The Seagull* or Gaev in *The Cherry Orchard* are often brutally silenced by the younger generation). But instead of the row ending with Serebriakov and Maria Vasilievna leaving the stage, a typically Chekhovian awkward silence is interposed. Chekhov invents a superbly banal and morbid interchange, worthy of Samuel Beckett, between Elena and Voinitsky: 'It's nice weather today [...]' *Pause* 'It's good weather for hanging yourself.' Marina and her poultry then pass backstage. The passion in Astrov's speech emerges from a pit of bathos.

Now Chekhov reintroduces the vodka motif: before Astrov begins his exhortations, a workman arrives to call him away to the factory – as he searches for his cap, he first asks for a glass of vodka and then makes his first tentative approach to Elena, inviting her to his forestry nursery. New light is shed on Astrov's character. Firstly he shows his human failings before his divine mission. Secondly he (and his author) make him a parody of comic characters in Ostrovsky's plays – Astrov's comparison of himself to a man with big moustaches but small abilities and his distracted searching phrase, 'Where then?' (*Gde uzh, kuda uzh?*) place him in a farcical role. (One eccentric touch, however, was removed by Stanislavsky in his director's copy: originally Voinitsky accuses Astrov of being a vegetarian, to which Astrov replies, 'Yes I consider it a sin to kill animals.') The speech that follows now has a new subtext; we can divine in Astrov the same desire to impress Elena that is expressed by Voinitsky's spectacular necktie. The habit of the new Chekhovian male (e.g. Trigorin in *The Seagull*) is to allure the female by his complaints and a recital of his obsessions. Astrov's speech is begun for him by Sonia, his ardent disciple, whereas in the final version of *The Wood Demon* it was parodied by his opponent, Voinitsky. Only Voinitsky's last words, of mock applause, are kept to stimulate Astrov to take over the appeal. This is the most authorial part of the play, the core of Chekhov's initial outline to Suvorin, culminating in the magnificent lyrical evocation: 'When I plant a birch and then see its green shoots, it swaying in the wind, my soul is full of pride.' Only now the sententious ending 'in the knowledge that I am helping God to create an organism' is cut and replaced by the arrival of a glass of vodka. The anticlimax makes the audience forgive being preached at, for, in accepting the vodka, the preacher shows his weaknesses. Incorporating Fiodor's failings into Astrov's idealism was Chekhov's most brilliant stroke. On this note of vodka and embarrassment, Astrov quits the stage, whereas the Wood Demon pointlessly stays on long after his bolt is shot, to the end of the scene.

Act 1 of *Uncle Vania* now quickly closes, condensing the argument of an unrequited lover in the last Scenes, 8 and 9, of Act 1 of *The Wood Demon*. Only Elena and Voinitsky's voices are now heard: the game of croquet in the background; Serebriakov's anxious jealous calls are cut. What is added is a new leitmotiv and the absurd. The leitmotiv is Elena's fear of being caught out, 'Quiet, you might be heard.' The absurd lies in the repetitive noise of everyday life – the counterpoint of Telegin strumming a polka on the guitar that has lain untouched until half way through the Act, and Maria Vasilievna (usually muttering, rustling paper, scratching her pencil) annotating her pamphlets. The romantic agony is thus mocked.

The new Act 1 is over a third shorter than the old, despite the addition of Marina and her opening scene with Astrov. Other additions make an impact out of all proportion to their length: the references to the sultry heat prepares us for the storm of Act 2; the grouping of males and females less in couples and more in two separate groups gives us a zoological insight into the struggle for hierarchy in the household; moreover, the ludicrous touches undermine the authority of Astrov's vision and Voinitsky's passion. Above all, the increase in pauses, from one to five, tells us about the failure of language to communicate, about the imprisonment of each individual in his or her own anxieties.

A Reading of *Uncle Vania*: Act 2

Like many of Chekhov's best acts, Act 2 of *The Wood Demon* takes place at night; integrating it into *Uncle Vania*, Chekhov had to make few changes other than those consistent with his reduction in the cast and the demotion of the saintly, loving Wood Demon to a flawed, unloving doctor. As a result, the Act is little shorter than its original version. Changes to darken the atmosphere are made, nevertheless. Here too the importance of food is reduced: the sideboard is no longer visible from the start of the Act, and the dining table is not mentioned. The first quarrel, between Serebriakov and Elena is transferred almost verbatim, the only cuts being to remove any details of the professor's past – his life in a cheap dirty rented room, working, starving, anguished at living at someone else's expense – that might make him seem more human, venerable or lovable. The second row with Sonia and the third with Voinitsky are also virtually unchanged, Sonia taking over just a few of Iulia's domestic virtues when she pleads the hay-making as a reason for her short temper.

The fourth episode of the Act, however, when Marina enters and succeeds in leading Serebriakov offstage to bed, radically alters the original Scene 4 of the Act in *The Wood Demon*: it is not the doctor/Wood Demon whose skill manoeuvres the childish old man away, but the subtle Marina, and her methods have a dark side not always noticed by the critics. She brings up the subject of the first Mrs Serebriakov, Vera Petrovna, apparently for no good reason; she reminds the professor of something we are never going to have explained, of Vera Petrovna's mental and physical agony: 'That's an old disease of yours. Vera Petrovna, God rest her soul, Sonia's mother, used not to sleep at night, she was in a terrible state…. She was very fond of you.' Restless corpses dominate mature Chekhovian drama, but not the early plays. We never know why the tyrannical Serebriakov can be tamed by a mention of his unhappy late wife, of whom nobody has a bad word to say, but we can suspect some guilty secret. Neither Sonia nor Elena ever mention her (just as the three sisters avoid mentioning their mother), giving us a hint of some unmentionable closet, from which the skeleton never falls. After this initial tack, Marina treats the professor as just another child to be sedated with lime tea and prayed for: the infantilism of the adult male is brought out in *Uncle Vania* even more strongly than in *The Wood Demon*. Scene 5 of Act 2 in *The Wood Demon* takes up the end of Act 1; like all the most dynamic scenes, Chekhov is able to use it with only minor revision in *Uncle Vania*. The revisions bring in repetitive phrases, for instance Elena's opening and closing remark, 'Things are unhappy in this house' and remove the moralising elements from both Voinitsky and Elena. In fact, Elena, despite her status as a passive, destructive element, is now given much of the prophetic role in the play: her 'Things are unhappy...' predicts the action of the next Act, just as she alone links the destruction of the forests to the devastation brought about in people's lives by the same greed and thoughtlessness. Now, however, the shock is greater, because we learn that it is the doctor, not Fiodor Orlovsky, who has got Voinitsky drunk, and our faith in the doctor, as the traditional fount of wisdom and goodness in the 19th-century play and novel, is badly damaged. At the same time as he gets rid of the traditional moral linch-pin, Chekhov removes from his plot the traditional motor of the plot, the melodramatic misunderstanding: in *The Wood Demon* the Wood Demon now misinterprets the scene he interrupts and accuses Elena and Voinitsky of moral corruption. The plot of *The Wood Demon* is creakily engineered by this calumny, for it is supposed to take Voinitsky to the point of suicide. Two orthodox ingredients of drama are thus dispensed with: a moral centre and a plot motor. The empty space is filled by moral and causal inconsequentiality.

What follows may seem the least convincing part of the play: Voinitsky's monologue, whether addressed to the audience or to the world at large. Strangely (if we believe Chekhov was moving towards more realistic drama), this monologue is enlarged, not cut. The first half gives the audience intriguing snippets of the information it has been starved of – the fact that ten years ago Voinitsky met Elena and that she had been a friend of his late sister, Vera Petrovna, that she is now 27 and he is 47. In the exclamation 'It was so possible!' it also preserves the last vestige of *The Wood Demon*'s references to Pushkin's and Tchaikovsky's *Eugene Onegin*, with Voinitsky's pursuit of Elena parodying Onegin's last approach to Tatiana. The second half of the monologue is now changed from envy of the Wood Demon's naïvety into a new escalation of hatred towards the professor. Serebriakov is now further lowered in our eyes, since all the evidence to defend him from Voinitsky's accusations of charlatanism and exploitation has been whittled away. Now the trading in vegetable oil, peas and curds which was the joy of Iulia Zheltukhina represents the hell of servitude into which Voinitsky and Sonia have been plunged by their enslavement to the professor. The rising hysteria which threatens to engulf Voinitsky is now motivation enough for a monologue without a collocutor: the device no longer seems artificial, whereas in *The Wood Demon* it seems a clumsy device belatedly to inform the audience. (Stanislavsky, however, fought shy of monologues, and in his 1899 production Voinitsky addresses the first half of his complaints not to the audience but to a silent Elena, and Chekhov's third-person pronouns are turned into 'you', 'your'. In Stanislavsky's version, only when Voinitsky's monologue attacks the professor does Elena then leave.)

The next Scene, 7 in *The Wood Demon*, now replaces Fiodor with the doctor and also demotes Diadin by having the doctor accompanied by Telegin (with guitar) as his clown. Astrov is given a few lines of a famous peasant drinking song, 'Move, hut, move stove, The master has no room to lie down.' Any Russian audience knows that the song then moves to ribaldry. If this were not enough to deconstruct the doctor as God, at the sight of the medicine drops that sparked off a row between Serebriakov and Sonia, Astrov then goes on to mock his patient and lust after his patient's wife – enough to have him struck off the register of any modern medical association. Chekhov gives him Fiodor Orlovsky's cynical motif – that a man can only be a woman's friend after he has been her lover – and completes it by adding Astrov's claim that he performs his most brilliant operations when drunk. Unlike the cosmopolitan Fiodor Orlovsky, who drinks chartreuse, the purely Russian Astrov offers his companions just brandy (*koniak*).

In his drunken arrogance, however, Astrov comes to resemble more the professor of medicine in *A Dreary Story*. The professor, disgusted by the obnoxious Gnekker, his prospective son-in-law, is overcome by a sense of superiority: 'my achievements in science seem to be a lofty mountain the top of which vanishes into the clouds, while at its foot Gnekkers are running about scarcely visible to the naked eye'; Astrov, when drunk, has his 'own philosophical system and all of you, brothers, seem to me to be just bugs...microbes.'

The third part of Act 2 in both plays centres on Sonia: the problem for Chekhov was to replace a fetching conversation between two *ingénus* in love with a cruel misunderstanding between the naïve Sonia and the world-weary Astrov. Dramatically, this was an opportunity to introduce the theatrical conflict that is so spectacularly absent from the first half of *The Wood Demon*. Sonia now begins, not by an offer of food, but by remonstrating with Astrov for getting Voinitsky drunk. Food and drink still punctuate their dialogue, but the counterpoint is now full of interesting discords. Many of the Wood Demon's best speeches are still kept: two of them have become clichés in the Russian intellectual's image of himself. The first is the statement, directed as criticism of Elena's idle beauty: 'Everything should be beautiful in a human being: face, clothes, soul and thoughts.' Almost every Soviet critic of Chekhov has reproduced this statement as if it came direct from Chekhov's mouth and not from a protagonist who is much narrower than his author, whether the character is naïve or cynical. Such aspirations may have been an article of faith for Chekhov, but the evidence of his life and letters does not show him as unequivocally idealistic as either the Wood Demon or Astrov. In any case, the *Uncle Vania* version of this affirmation is much coarsened by the addition of the reproach: 'She only eats, sleeps and walks', a list of basic human functions which is to recur as a mark of male disgust in all the late plays.

The second cliché, also much misattributed to Chekhov himself, is the Wood Demon's and doctor's speech comparing life to a journey through a dark forest of thorns with no light in the distance. Here Chekhov radically alters the speech: the Wood Demon announces that he has found the flame that lights his way through the woods – love. The whole point of Astrov's characterisation, however, lies in the change: 'But I have no distant flame to light my path.'

The comic misunderstanding in *The Wood Demon* is of little import, for the audience is quite clear that a happy ending to Sonia's and the Wood Demon's love is likely. Now love is not merely misunderstood, but explicitly unrequited, and Astrov's strategy to counter Sonia's questioning is sheer comic evasion. No longer does he moralise: he will do anything to make a quick getaway, even promise to stop drinking vodka – an undertaking to be brazenly broken in Act 4. The scene in *The Wood Demon* is unconvincing. We cannot understand why the couple should quarrel over a matter of priorities, nor why the Wood Demon should seem so insecure about others' opinion of him. In *Uncle Vania* Astrov emerges more plausibly as a damaged misanthropist, who can feel affection only for the old nurse and can feel only lust for attractive women. Sonia's reaction as her beloved departs seems perverse in *The Wood Demon*. In *Uncle Vania* her mixture of delight at her own courage and despair at her ugliness is psychologically utterly convincing.

For a brief moment Sonia is left alone to lament. Stanislavsky in his 1899 production completely cut her monologue which ends 'I'm ugly.' But by making Sonia ugly – an obvious explanation of Astrov's indifference to her which not every actress or director has been willing to accept – the next scene with the entry of the beautiful, idle Elena gains in dramatic contrast. The sharp opposition of two types of female – active, unattractive in black, and inert, beautiful in white – began in *The Seagull* and is used in all late Chekhov. It represents a dualism of women as predators and victims in Chekhov's mature work. The reduced cast of characters acquires symbolic value.

Some of the brilliance of the closing scene of Act 2 is already there in *The Wood Demon*: Elena enters with the theme of the open window which she had fought to shut in the beginning of the Act. Now she opens the window and announces the passing of the storm. The audience only becomes aware of the war between the two women, who have not yet exchanged a word, now that they make peace. Elena makes an avowal – but

mystifying, rather than enlightening the audience in the cynical light of
Uncle Vania – when she declares that she married the professor for love.
However, where *The Wood Demon* continues with Elena's defence of
Serebriakov, Chekhov changes tack in *Uncle Vania*: Elena's silence on her
husband's merits is eloquent and makes her praise of the doctor far more
ambiguous than her unstinted and disinterested praise of the Wood Demon.
The reconciliation of stepmother and stepdaughter, however, is discordantly
counterpointed by their gestures: while Elena, upset, paces the room like
the caged bird she compares herself to, Sonia, static, covers her face
with happiness. Their dialogue often separates into two simultaneous
monologues: the conciliation is superficial only. (In Stanislavsky's direction,
however, the two women 'both drink water, wave their handkerchiefs about,
sigh, blow their noses. Traces of emotion, breathlessness, tears – voices
shake. Elena dampens her handkerchief and wipes her temples.') The
ending, however, with an embrace which is to be consecrated by a piano
recital, is the same as in *The Wood Demon*: Serebriakov sends a message
through Sonia forbidding them to play the piano. The unplayed piano,
however, is to be used far more effectively in the next act of *Uncle Vania*
than in *The Wood Demon*.

A Reading of *Uncle Vania*: Act 3

The drawing room of the Serebriakov-Voinitsky household remains the scene for Act 3. But the first half of Act 3 of *Uncle Vania* had to be completely rewritten: much of its action was lost with the playwright's elimination of Fiodor and the Zheltukhins. Chekhov's main change is to remove the Wood Demon from the second half of the act and to give him a spectacularly central role in the first half, in a scene that blends farce and sermon with a virtuosity which Chekhov never attempted again and which no dramatist has ever since rivalled.

Instead of the original transparent opening, with Elena offstage playing Lensky's aria on the piano and Voinitsky announcing that this suicidal piece is his favourite piece of music, Chekhov (at least as Stanislavsky set the scene) now has a large grand piano standing centre stage, in eloquent silence, as Elena paces the stage and Voinitsky and Sonia sit and watch her. Now, deprived of operatic allusion, the action is tautened: Voinitsky's opening line announces Serebriakov's imminent entry together with the rest of the household in 15 minutes' time. Note how real time (as measured on the audience's watches) coincides with stage time, a rare phenomenon in the European theatre until Chekhov's late plays. Hitherto dramatists avoid mentioning time, lest the artificial pace on stage be noticed. Time, however, is a force, even a character, in late Chekhov, and its progress is constantly monitored by the time-wasting characters whom it in turn will waste.

In this new version, very little of the early part of Act 3 is preserved. Only the comments on Elena's idleness and her irritated response to them are kept. The water-nymph (*rusalka*), which Voinitsky urges is the true character of Elena, fits with the folklore and water imagery that permeates *The Wood Demon*; in *Uncle Vania*, however, it just seems another inept device by which Voinitsky hopes to attract Elena's sympathy. In *The Wood Demon* Elena consents to this image, calling herself a 'free bird, flying far away from you.' Her descent from Homer's Helen of Troy or Offenbach's *La belle Hélène* is implied by her reasons for staying faithful: 'if all wives followed my example and abandoned their husbands, God would punish me....' In *Uncle Vania* these poetic and mythological overtones are erased: deprived of her crowd of admirers, in the reduced company of this play, we are left with just an inadequate, unhappy, cowardly and isolated stranger.

Now the time scale is more specific and more cruel as to the season, as well as the hour: it is September, as opposed to the May in which the play opened (a month marked by the early dawn of Act 2). The sense of ineluctable time spreads from character to character – again, a feature of late Chekhovian drama: Voinitsky's promise of 'Autumn roses – charming, sad roses', appropriately from a prose poem in Turgenev's *Senilia* – sets up an echo. Sonia repeats the phrase, both women look out of the window and Elena in horror exclaims, 'Somehow we shall live out the winter here!' Elena's desperation, in which she longs to fly away like a bird from the sleepy faces around her, would be moving, were it not for the echo of so many Chekhovian misfits, for example, the first version (1886) of the farcical monologue *On the harmfulness of tobacco*, where Chekhov's hero Niukhin (= 'sniffer') also longs 'to run away without turning round'.

But Elena's predatory instinct reasserts itself: seeing Sonia provokes her, as in Act 2 to ask, 'Where is the doctor?' The negotiations between Sonia and Elena that ended Act 2 are now restarted. This is far cleverer dialogue than the conversation between the female characters in Scenes 5 and 6 of Act 3 in *The Wood Demon*. Only in *The Seagull* had Chekhov found a way of conveying the subtle wrangling underlying women's dialogue with women. This new passage he devised for *Uncle Vania* very cleverly shows Elena's ruthless, subconscious pursuit of her own goal beneath her apparently altruistic offer of assistance to Sonia.

Once again, Chekhov reverts to monologue, but whereas Elena's short monologue in *The Wood Demon* is a stagey reaction to a mysterious letter from Voinitsky that Sonia has found in the garden (in the well-worn theatrical tradition of fortuitous finds), here we have an extended monologue that poetically echoes words that Elena could not possibly have heard. In Act 2 Astrov complains that Elena only 'eats, sleeps, walks...'. Now she describes the house in the same hellish terms as 'desperate boredom, when instead of human beings grey spots wander about, you hear only trivialities, when they only know that they eat, drink, sleep...'. The colour grey typifies the closed world of the Chekhovian heroine: Elena's complaint anticipates the despair of the Lady with the little dog in the story of that name, and explains (as in the story) her susceptibility to the cynical enchanter who now appears.

Astrov's appearance with his maps of the district's ecology is one of Chekhov's classic stage jokes.[4] Never in his stories or plays, even in his journalism, did Chekhov preach at such length as Astrov. The comic effect of stopping the action lies entirely in Elena's amazed reaction: showing her the maps, the pretext for an encounter, appears to be the sole and real reason for their meeting.

The text for Astrov's speech grows out of a few lines in Act 4, Scene 6 of *The Wood Demon*, where the Wood Demon explains to Sonia that he is mapping the local forests, not drawing, and that it would bore her. Now there are three maps, all dealing not just with the region, but with the times: 50 years ago, 25 years ago and now. If a new force has been introduced into the play, it is certainly time, for the passage of centuries (in Act 1), hours (in Act 2), minutes, months and years (Act 3 and 4) is harped on as it never was in *The Wood Demon*.

In writing Astrov's conservation speech Chekhov must have turned to the stories he had written in late 1887, just before beginning *The Wood Demon*. Not just the general tone and imagery of the speech, but specific phrases are to be found in stories such as *Panpipes*. The narrative in this story begins with the Wood Demon's motif of the young birch tree; then the ranch-manager Meliton complains that for over 40 years the birds have been dying out, that once they had been more than the eye could take in (*vidimo-nevidimo*) – exactly the same flocks of birds *vidimo-nevidimo* that Astrov cites. Although Meliton's country idiolect is very different from Astrov's educated exposition, he ends with the same message warning about the senseless destruction: compare his 'Whatever grows, they hack it down, so without end until nothing more is left.' to Astrov's 'A frozen hungry sick human being [...] destroys everything, not thinking of the morrow. Almost everything is now destroyed.'

In recycling the material of his earlier story Chekhov is raising dialogue from narrative to drama, and also raising the language from peasant to intellectual register. Many of Astrov's phrases betray his university education much more subtly than the Wood Demon's: he talks of 'degeneration', of 'struggle for existence', a neo-Darwinian vocabulary with which Chekhov had endowed his ruthless scientist-protagonist Von Koren in *The Duel* (1891). But this vocabulary also stems from the wide reading of ecological literature, from Thoreau's *Walden* to Élisée Reclus's *La Terre*,[5] that had sharpened Chekhov's views in the early 1890s and made him their rival as a pioneering ecologist.

The incongruity of Astrov's ecological passion and Elena's selfish boredom is made shatteringly obvious when he catches her eye, realises where her real interest lies and forcefully dismisses her enquiries about his intentions towards Sonia. His passionate kiss and the entry of Voinitsky at that worst possible moment with a bunch of roses makes the end of the episode a farcical scene as skilful as any of Feydeau's. The overall effect, however, is to leave Elena fraught (and a few minutes later) Sonia equally distressed, when she realises Elena's mission to Astrov has failed. The play has now built up enough tension to make Serebriakov's much heralded announcement a disaster. In *The Wood Demon* Chekhov had tried to build up the same tension by having Elena pestered by Fiodor Orlovsky, but her indignation there is nothing compared to the embarrassment, confusion, public humiliation and repressed desire she is made silently to contain in *Uncle Vania*.

From Serebriakov's entry to the catastrophic end of the Act, Chekhov used the material of the earlier play fairly closely. Orlovsky's complaints of illness are given to Telegin; the humour is heightened by having Elena present, but unnoticed by Serebriakov when he calls her with the rest of the assembly to order, while his own daughter cannot hear him. The alienation of the old man, from a wife he cannot see and a daughter whose attention he cannot catch, is complete. Thus when Voinitsky addresses Serebriakov with the formal *vy* instead of the intimate *ty* we realise that the household has distanced itself from its head, and the older generation – the professor and his mother-in-law – is frozen out of their concern.

Like Astrov's speech, Serebriakov's speech would be undramatic were it not for the aghast reception that its listeners give it. The new version is almost identical to the old: in order to bring it to a perfection of pompous menace, Chekhov had only to tamper with a few details – Serebriakov's sale of timber – and with the pauses. Scene 11 of *The Wood Demon*, where Diadin has considerably more to say than Telegin is permitted, had to be cut more severely, particularly his invitation to picnic at the water mill. But the attempt to pour oil on water in both plays only makes the flames of hatred flare brighter.[6] Other elements, too, are subtly heightened. When Voinitsky protests that the estate is not Serebriakov's to sell, that it was part of his sister's dowry, to which he sacrificed his share, his reference to the dead Vera Petrovna becomes more emotional: 'my sister whom I loved' is now 'my sister whom I loved fervently.' Similarly, his fury at the 25 years wasted worshipping Serebriakov is heightened by the simple addition: 'You made fools of us.'

The end of the row, however, is very different: Sonia intervenes at length to appeal to her father's better nature, while Marina sits imperturbably knitting her stocking, resembling both one of the Parcæ unravelling some-body's fate and the spirit of serenity to which Sonia clings. Her sudden wrath, the transition from talking of lime tea or raspberry tea to cursing the quarrelling ganders, marks a real change in the play's atmosphere. While *The Wood Demon* has the Wood Demon enter to plead with Serebriakov to save the forests, *Uncle Vania* proceeds straight to the dénouement with a shot offstage and a shot onstage. The first shot we might assume to be the same as before in Chekhov's plays centering on a male hero – suicide being the end of Platonov, Ivanov and, in *The Seagull*, Treplev. (One might suspect that in 1896 Chekhov had decided that suicide was too easy an answer in drama as in life, for after *The Seagull* he never uses suicide in the plots of his plays and only once more in his stories, namely in *On Official Business*.) But the reappearance of Voinitsky in the doorway, firing nearly point blank and yet missing his target, mingles tragedy and farce and the act closes on a static scene of howling women, not on Elena asking Diadin to take her away. The earlier play promises a new location and makes room for an Act 4 in which something more must happen: by killing a central figure in Act 3, Chekhov appears to have shot his dramatic bolt, but at the same time left us needing a solution. Now, with a farcical and horribly inconclusive rupture of all social norms, Chekhov has left nothing to resolve. The Act to follow this had to be something totally new in the history of drama.

A Reading of *Uncle Vania*: Act 4

Act 4 is the failure of *The Wood Demon* and the success of *Uncle Vania*. Chekhov's well-known remark to Suvorin in 1892 shows how aware he was of the importance of an ending: 'Anyone who invents new endings for a play will open a new era. Vile endings don't work! The hero either gets married or shoots himself, there is no other way out [...] I shan't write the comedy until I think of an ending as ingenious (*zakovyristy*) as the beginning.' In *The Wood Demon* Chekhov had tried to have a new ending, by bringing the catastrophe forward to Act 3 and demoting Act 4 to an aftermath. Even *The Seagull* had reverted, however, to the traditional shock ending. The achievement of *Uncle Vania* is to invent what Thomas Winner (1966) has called the 'zero-ending'.[7] To do so meant writing almost totally new material. The only feature of the old Act 4 that Chekhov preserves are the frequent pauses. Only a few phrases are left over from the original. After three acts set in the space allocated to the rest of the household, we are finally confined in Voinitsky's quarters – office, bedroom and junk-room at once. The imagery of the earlier action – the trade in agricultural products, the caged bird which Elena believes herself to be – is all realised here in concrete form. As well as the scales, ledgers, and the starling in a cage[8] Chekhov adds apparently gratuitous props whose purpose must puzzle the audience – notably the map of Africa 'of no use to anyone' on the wall.

In the opening scene Telegin and Marina laugh at the events of Act 3. They reassure the audience that there have been no consequences. However different the disaster – suicide or attempted murder – in both plays Chekhov horrifies his audience with the inconsequential aftermath, whether the surviving characters reconcile or depart. But this is a ludicrous, not a happy ending. Marina's knitting of Act 3 has developed into wool-winding and enveloped Telegin, taking the parody of the Parcæ spinning, measuring and cutting lifelines to a ludicrous extreme. Only a few of Diadin's exclamations, notably 'A subject worthy of Aivazovsky's brush' and 'Fatal predetermination', are kept in Telegin's responses. By demoting the independent Diadin to the dependent Telegin Chekhov has made him one of the servants and has written a scene familiar to traditional comedy: the irreverent 'downstairs' comments on the high drama 'upstairs'. The furious heroes are still just cackling ganders to Marina. Yet a note of melancholy is introduced

56

that takes us back to Act 1: Marina's lament, 'I haven't had noodles for a long time', echoes her complaints at the decline in the household, while Telegin, recalling how bitter he felt when the village shopkeeper mocked him, takes us back to the sad account in Act 1 of his wife leaving him on his wedding night.

The musical, cyclic construction of the play, which we first encountered in *The Seagull* with Act 4 recalling phrases and moods of Act 1, is now established as the mark of mature Chekhovian drama: in its end is its beginning. In *Uncle Vania* this cyclic element is even more prominent than in *The Seagull*, for no death has occurred to alter the fundamental structure of the characters' relationships. The only really new factor is that we now have a geographical co-ordinate: the Serebriakovs have decided to flee to Kharkov, a town which also figures at the end of *A Dreary Story*, where it typifies the provincial squalor in which the disillusioned professor faces up to his imminent death.[9]

The relaxed Diadin in *The Wood Demon* is merely astounded by the Wood Demon's rushed entry; now Telegin and Marina leave the stage to make for Astrov in a very new mood – merciless rage with Voinitsky whom he threatens with violence because he suspects he has stolen his morphine. A doctor who now advises his depressed patient to take a gun and shoot himself in the forest is the ultimate anti-therapist, and the deconstruction of that saintly cliché in Turgenev's *A Month in the Country*[10] or in Chekhov's own prose, the noble doctor, is now complete. Perhaps Astrov's brutal abuse of Voinitsky is shock therapy: undoubtedly affection breaks through the exasperation towards the end of the episode. There is an astonishing diapason from fury to pity in this dialogue of the deaf in which the distressed Voinitsky continues to lament in the infantile tones of the previous acts, 'If you only knew', being his favourite phrase.

Two of Voinitsky's sentences are taken from the Wood Demon's speech to Serebriakov, in Act 3, Scene 13 of *The Wood Demon*. In *The Wood Demon* he was defending his own sanity against Serebriakov's accusations when he sarcastically protests: 'Mad people are not those who hide their cruel, stony hearts as scholarliness, and pretend their lack of soul is deep wisdom. Mad people are not those who marry old men only to deceive them in front of everybody.' This is now far more effective as part of Voinitsky's proclamation of a Trojan war: his insane attack on the men who have deprived him of his Elena. The difference between the madman and the eccentric (*chudak*) around which this row revolves – Astrov insists that Voinitsky is just another *chudak* and denies him or the other characters the dignity or the irresponsibility of clinical insanity – now amounts to one of the chief themes of *Uncle Vania*, for, like the Wood Demon, Astrov considers himself a *chudak* and yet is called by some a psychopath or a 'fool in Christ' (*iurodivy*). Once he calls Voinitsky a *chudak*, he recognises their brotherhood again, and the row becomes a chorus of numbers, like their first conversation in Act 1. The difference is that Voinitsky counts time in years: thirteen years of hell, from 47 now to death at 60,[11] while Astrov as in Act 1 thinks in centuries and eternity – the sane life that will come in 100 or 200 years, or the dreams he and Voinitsky will dream in their coffins. From Chekhov's early journalism to the last speeches of *The Cherry Orchard*, the idealist talking of the happy centuries to come is imbued with authorial irony at the expense of all ragged idealists. It is a crude misreading of Chekhov to identify the Act 4 'evolutionary optimist' Astrov as closely with the author as the Act 3 ecologist Astrov. He is showing how the male of the species uses time to pace himself, some by the hour (like Serebriakov timing the day by his watch), some by the year (Voinitsky measuring his nostalgia and his horror of ageing), some by the century (Astrov and the glorious future whose notional trail he is blazing). Even if it is not definitively authorial, however, Astrov's vision is the only element in the play that stretches beyond the action, and its distant optimism is belied by the eloquence of his Beckettian pessimism about the immediate prospects: 'The only hope [you and I have] is that when we lie in our coffins we will be visited by visions that may even be pleasant.' Astrov's references to the district make it a symbol not just of ecological degeneration but of spiritual wasteland – quite in contrast to the well-watered, luxuriant Ukrainian landscape of *The Wood Demon*. This is a district in which only two decent men existed (Voinitsky and Astrov) and they in the last ten years so crucial to the action of this play – note, the ten years since Vera Petrovna died – have been dragged down to its 'banal, despicable' level. Voinitsky's moral death, not to mention the rejection that his niece Sonia meets, perhaps is even more fatal a blow to the genteel line of the Voinitskys than was the suicide of Uncle Zhorzh in *The Wood Demon*. We have here the victory of the petty bourgeois – the *meshchanin* or *obyvatel'* – over the declining aristocrat, which is so typical of Russian literature in the second half of the 19th century and of Chekhov's late drama, culminating in Natasha's usurpation of the house and position of the *Three Sisters* and in Lopakhin's purchase of the cherry orchard and dispersal of its original owners. At least in *The Wood Demon* there was the possibility of male progeny to continue the line: from *The Seagull* onwards the gentry are condemned to extinction, together with nature that was once their estate.

In the course of this last act a typical Chekhovian bunching occurs: the characters who are stranded (like the three sisters) gather together, and those who are to depart congregate separately. Thus Sonia enters to take control of Voinitsky, while Astrov and Elena negotiate their own farewell; Astrov's mood switches from rage to playful cynicism, a mood to which Elena easily responds so that we can agree with Astrov's prediction that she will eventually succumb to a love affair – in a hotel room in Kharkov, rather than the lap of nature here.[12] The sexual undercurrents in their leave-taking are symbolised (in a touch Thomas Mann was to use in *The Magic Mountain*) by Elena taking one of Astrov's pencils as a souvenir of the encounter. The significance of the gesture is understood by both of them, as a peck on the cheek turns into a brief but 'impulsive' (*poryvisty*) embrace.

Here we have the first of many 'false endings'. Like *The Cherry Orchard*, the play tails off deceptively, and there are half a dozen points at which the curtain could fall: Astrov's comments *Finita la commedia!...Finita!* could apply to more than his own private comedy. It could be the end of the entire play. But Serebriakov then enters in an apologetic mood for the nearest this act approaches to conciliation: consequently, Chekhov can use some of the material of Act 4 of *The Wood Demon*. What Serebriakov says to the Wood Demon he now addresses to Voinitsky: he has 'learnt so much that he could write for posterity a whole edifying treatise on how to live.' The apology has lost any nobility it may once have had now that it is addressed not to the doctor, but to the oppressed brother-in-law at whose expense and on whose labour the professor proposes to go on living. Diadin's clichés 'Whoever remembers grudges, may he lose his eye', are also transferred to Serebriakov. If Act 4 of *The Wood Demon* preaches apology and forgiveness with apparent sincerity in the hope of a new era of honest relationships, in *Uncle Vania* the preaching is a mere formality to allow the old injustice and lies to be perpetuated. The play seems to have run full circle: the defeated Voinitsky tells his enemy that 'Everything will be as it was' (*po-staromu*, as of old); Serebriakov reverts to type with his pompous and palpably insincere insistence that 'Deeds not thoughts count' (*Nado delo delat'*). Voinitsky takes his last farewell of Elena.

But the audience knows that, beneath the surface economic relations, nothing can be 'as of old': the disillusion of Voinitsky and departure of Astrov from both Elena's and Sonia's lives are irreversible. Note, however, that as in Act 1, Sonia no longer speaks to Elena: the step-mother has resumed her role as the unspeakable, unforgivable alien, and the symmetry of leave-taking is disrupted by their refusal to notice each other. For a second time the play could, but does not, end. Astrov and Voinitsky are joined by Marina and her knitting. The word *uekhali* ('they've left') echoes from character to character – Marina, Sonia, even Maria Vasilievna all enter with perhaps undisguised relief at the departure of their tormentors. A static scene of knitting, accounting, reading and packing seems a third opportunity for the curtain to fall.

Then a new incident spoils the harmony: as Astrov takes his leave he accepts what he first refused then asked for in Act 1, and what he renounced in Act 2: a glass of vodka. Sonia's final betrayal is conveyed in the embarrassed pause as he waits for the vodka, at which point he makes two apparently casual remarks: firstly that his horse has gone lame – as significant an admission as *The Cherry Orchard*'s broken thermometer that Varia mentions in her final non-proposal scene to Lopakhin. Secondly, the prop on the wall, hitherto as cryptic as the writing at Balshazzar's feast, comes into force as Astrov remarks, 'The heat in that Africa there must be really terrible' – which we can interpret as a hint at the torment burning Sonia's soul, or at the warmth that Astrov is to desert for solitude and a cold winter outside. The device strikes the heart of each spectator's complexes: no wonder Gorky wrote to Chekhov, 'When Astrov started talking about Africa, I quivered with ecstasy at the strength of your talent.' (Stanislavsky gave the episode special attention when he acted the part of Astrov. 'How much bitterness and experience of life he put into this phrase. And how he uttered these words with an almost provocative bravura,' commented Olga Knipper.)

Again *uekhal* ('he's left') echoes from Marina to Sonia, and again the curtain fails to fall. Telegin's entry begins a drawn out coda, the first fully musical end in Chekhov's work, for not only does the play die away, recapitulating all its themes, but the last dialogue takes place to the accompaniment of Telegin tuning his guitar. Here Chekhov anticipates the coda of the *Three Sisters* where the bleakness of the heroines' utter abandonment is dressed in a mystical vision conjured up to defy reality. Few passages in the dramatic theatre have been so frequently and so wilfully misdirected. In no way is Sonia's vision of ultimate justice and happiness authorial, any more than that of the three sisters: this is a female strategy for facing the future. It is here also a device for silencing Voinitsky's tears, for Voinitsky once again has lapsed into infantile sobbing with only fairytales about a world beyond the grave with 'a bright, beautiful, elegant life' to compensate. To the motifs of 'work' and 'coffin' that has echoed, Sonia now adds a new word, 'we shall rest' (*otdokhniom*), that the *Three Sisters* also saves for its coda. The musicality of Sonia's improvisation, its rhythmic arrangement of images, is as near to free verse as Chekhov ever came. (Rachmaninov recognised this when he chose to set Chekhov's text as a song, 'We shall rest'.) At this fifth and final cadence the curtain falls, and both the lighting and the banging of the night-watchman in the garden remind us that we are now in an autumn night, even more dismal than the brief stormy summer night of Act 2. If Act 2 led from night to dawn, this Act 4 ends in undissipated gloom: the sun has set for a very long time indeed.

The new Act 4 resembles Act 2, not just because it is a nocturne, but because of its economy, its avoidance of mass scenes. (It is less than half the length of Act 4 of *The Wood Demon*, and shorter than any other Act of the play.) Stanislavsky underlined its brilliance and its novelty when he later complained that it was interchangeable with Act 4 of *The Cherry Orchard*. The dramatic events in both plays conclude Act 3, so that Act 4 is a reversion to Act 1, and a reversal, since the departures mirror the arrivals, and the patterns of relationships that developed in Acts 2 and 3 revert to those of Act 1.

The Reception of *Uncle Vania*

Our own critical interpretation of *Uncle Vania* can only build on the Russian public's reception, at first bemused, then enthusiastic, of the work. Three factors inhibited the response: firstly the play was published two years before it was first performed in Moscow 26 October 1899 (even though it had had a number of provincial performances from 1897); secondly, although *The Wood Demon* had been read and seen by only a few hundred people, it was widely known that the new play was a reworking of its lame prototype; thirdly *The Seagull*, which was published in the same 1897 edition of Chekhov's collected plays, was still recovering its reputation from its disappointing first staging in St Petersburg. It was not until the triumphant Moscow Arts Theatre performance of autumn 1898 that Chekhov's reputation as a great playwright became permanently unassailable.

The first critics responded to the written text, which they found far less interesting than such controversial stories as *Peasants*. They were sceptical about its viability on the stage: 'Seven or eight years ago the same play, as *The Wood Demon*, was performed on one of the Moscow private stages [...] Now the drama, or as the author modestly calls it, "Scenes from country life" has been significantly reworked [...] The impression from reading the play is very great and very depressing, oppressive. It is difficult to predict its success on the stage. Even after reworking it is unlikely to find success with the average spectator [...] Much is vaguely sketched, the whole action seems to be wrapped in mist, perhaps deliberately. You have to give it a lot of thought to understand the motives behind the heroes' actions and evaluate all the truth in them. But spectators like clarity, precision, definition, firm, even sharp contours. So-called "mood" (and there is no end to the mood in the play!) is valued very little in the auditorium.' (*Novosti dnia*, 5 June 1897).

Such opinions kept *Uncle Vania* off the metropolitan stage. In May 1897 Chekhov's friend Sumbatov-Iuzhin offered to have it or *The Seagull* staged by the Moscow Maly Theatre: but it was not until February 1899 that the acting director of the Maly formally asked for the performing rights and only then did the Theatrical-Literary Committee meet at the home of the director of the Moscow office of Russia's Imperial Theatres for a reading. The actors present loved the play; the bureaucrats on the committee (including I.I.

Ivanov who had loathed *The Wood Demon*) insulted the author and damned
the play by demanding revisions: 'we recognise it as deserving of production on condition that minor cuts and revisions are carried out in accordance
with the indications of the Committee's department and a second submis-
sion to the Committee.' Unfortunately, Nemirovich-Danchenko felt that as
director of the Moscow Arts Theatre he could not allow a conflict of interests
to arise by attending and swinging the committee's verdict by his single
vote.

The committee sent Chekhov a more substantial, if obtuse, critique:

> Its staging has certain unevenness or gaps. Before Act 3
> Uncle Vania and Astrov seem to merge into the type of
> failure, superfluous man which is fairly successfully
> sketched in Mr Chekhov's works. Nothing prepares us for
> that powerful burst of passion which occurs during his talk
> with Elena[13] [...] That Voinitsky might take a dislike to the
> professor as Elena's husband is understandable [...] but
> disillusion in Serebriakov's greatness as a scholar, especially
> as an art historian is somewhat strange [...] is no excuse for
> pursuing him firing a pistol, chasing him like a madman. If
> the spectator were to link this state with the drunken state in
> which the author for some reason too often portrays both
> Uncle Vania and Astrov, the unpleasant and unexpected
> introduction of these two shots into the play takes on a
> peculiar and undesirable nuance. The character of Elena
> might need somewhat more clarification [...] Perhaps the
> main female character on the stage, the cause of so many
> alarms and dramas, endowed with a 'tiresome' character, she
> arouses no interest in the spectator. The play has longueurs,
> from a literary point of view these drag out the action with
> no profit to it. One instance is the protracted praise of forests
> in Act 1, shared by Sonia and Astrov, and the explanation of
> Astrov's theory of afforestation, so is the explanation of the
> maps, so is even the finely conceived depiction of the peace
> that falls after Elena and her husband have left, in the end of
> the play, and Sonia's dreams. In this final scene which comes
> after the main dramatic interest is exhausted the contrast
> should have been reduced to brief, bare essentials.

In April Chekhov visited one committee member, Teliakovsky, after this
letter for a 'conversation'. The latter recalls: 'Chekhov was absolute *sang-
froid*. He asked me not to fuss about his play being blackballed, said that of
course he would change nothing in the play [...] and to calm me promised

to write a new play by autumn specially for the Maly.' Thus, thanks to the conservatism of the Imperial theatres,[14] Stanislavsky and Nemirovich-Danchenko were presented with the play they had hoped for to consolidate the success of their production of *The Seagull*.

Meanwhile *Uncle Vania* was winning a shadowy provincial popularity. We know that it was performed in Kazan in October 1897 and with great success in Pavlovsk (the summer resort of many Petersburgers) in 1898. In autumn it played in Odessa and Kiev (a staging that Chekhov saw a few years later). Chekhov read the play to amateur actors who performed it in Serpukhov, a few miles from Melikhovo. In November it played in Chekhov's home town, Taganrog, where his cousin reported 'especially great success'. Nizhnii Novgorod, and Tiflis were other centres important enough to force Moscow and St Petersburg critics to take note of provincial reactions to what they had spurned. A critic who saw the Pavlovsk production already noted the Act 4 as 'a stage chef-d'œuvre' which made the play 'the most impressive work on the stage of recent years.' The Russian-language press in Tiflis (*Kavkaz*, 2 May 1899) showed the heartfelt empathy which provincial and colonial audiences in the Russian audience were to accord all the later Chekhovian drama, as if Chekhov were the first metropolitan writer to understand the dreary hopelessness of their lives on the fringe: 'in a truly Chekhovian way, that is with fine observation and deep psychological analysis [...] we see clever, talented, educated people spending their whole lives on trivia and withering in unconscious quietism, busy with things that are beneath them, gradually sucked into base trivial lives, existing with no profit to others or themselves.'

One perceptive Chekhovian stood alone: A.I. Urusov stood by his fondness for *The Wood Demon*. 'I have carefully reread *Uncle Vania* and must with sadness tell you that in my opinion you have ruined *The Wood Demon*. You have crumpled it, reduced it to an outline and disfigured it. You had a splendid comic villain: he has vanished, and he was necessary to the internal symmetry, and rogues of that stature, with luxuriant and bright plumage, is what you are especially good at. It was precious to the play, bringing in a humorous note. The second sin, in my view, is still more heinous: changing the pace of the play. The suicide in Act 3 and the nocturnal scene by the river with the tea table in Act 4, the wife's return to the doctor – all that was newer, bolder, more interesting than the end you have now. When I was retelling *The Wood Demon* to the French, it was this that struck them: the hero is killed, but life goes on. The actors I spoke to were of the same opinion. Of course, *Uncle Vania* is good, better than anything being written now – but *The Wood Demon* was better' (letter to Chekhov, 27 i 99).

One might also take Tolstoy's play *A Living Corpse* of 1900 as expressing a marked preference for *The Wood Demon* over *Uncle Vania*: Tolstoy's wayward hero, after his fictitious death is exposed, shoots himself so that his wife may marry a man worthy of her love, a plot which seems to turn the suicide of Voinitsky and reconciliation of the Serebriakovs into a morally coherent sequence, however much it may seem to be at odds with the asceticism preached elsewhere by Tolstoy. The failure of *The Wood Demon* continued to haunt *Uncle Vania*: when in 1901 the Society of Russian Playwrights and Opera Composers was deciding what play to recommend as the outstanding play of the previous year for the Griboyedov prize, they refused to consider *Uncle Vania* on the grounds that it was 'an adaptation of the same author's *The Wood Demon* which had already been considered.'

In Spring 1899 Nemirovich-Danchenko was glad to accept *Uncle Vania* for the Moscow Arts Theatre with no changes: Nemirovich-Danchenko directed (Stanislavsky was too busy preparing A.K. Tolstoy's *The Death of Ivan the Terrible*). Nemirovich-Danchenko persuaded Stanislavsky to play Astrov, although the latter's first preference was the title role.[15] Chekhov was present at one rehearsal of two acts in May and intervened to supply maps of Serpukhov with Melikhovo at the centre for Act 3. Chekhov was laconic, even cryptic, to any actor who asked him for help in interpreting a role: 'It's all written there,' was his standard reply. Only questions of dress – especially Vania's splendid tie – were expanded on by the author. The remaining rehearsals went on in Chekhov's absence, but with Nemirovich-Danchenko, Meierkhold and Olga Knipper all giving the playwright slightly varying accounts of the play's progress. Except for Knipper, the final casting corresponded not at all with Chekhov's original preferences, particularly for Komissarzhevskaia as Sonia and Davydov (who had acted in *The Wood Demon*) as Voinitsky. Stanislavsky's wife, Lilina, took Sonia, while Vishnevsky, who played Voinitsky, was probably the only actor whom Chekhov wholeheartedly trusted to interpret his part intelligently. As the theatre's co-director, and as Astrov on stage, Stanislavsky had more influence than Chekhov over Knipper's interpretation of Elena: 'For a greater difference from Arkadina, I'd give Elena – of course in the quiet places – more immobility, drawl, idleness, reserve and worldliness and, at the same time, I'd give more shadow to her temperament.' Their co-operation was close: Knipper confessed, 'When I felt [Astrov's] infatuated gaze, full of cunning, and heard his caressing irony, "You're cunning", I was always annoyed with that "intellectual" Elena for not going to visit him in his forest nursery.'

Meanwhile illness had forced Chekhov to retire to Yalta, from where he wrote to Vishnevsky (8 x 99): 'How upset and annoyed I am that I can't be with you all, that I am missing almost all rehearsals and the performances and know them only at second hand, whereas it would be enough for me to be present at rehearsals to recharge myself, to get experience and get down to a new play.'

The production appears to have been an outstanding success. Nemirovich-Danchenko's and Stanislavsky's production copy[16] gives some hint of the care and ingenuity with which they realised Chekhov's directions and of their contribution to the play's success. (See Tables 1-4 for a schematic reproduction of Stanislavsky's own sketches for each act.) The greenery of the opening scene went far beyond Chekhov's specifications. For Act 1 Stanislavsky specified mosquitoes, real chickens for Marina to round up, and even a dog. In creating the mood he specified that Astrov should smoke with a long cigarette holder and roll his own *papirosy*, while Voinitsky was to appear in a dressing-gown, and Maria Vasilievna with both pince-nez and lorgnette with a handbag full of pencils. The prop list for Act 2 was likewise inventive: hot water bottles were added to Serebriakov's medicines. As with *The Cherry Orchard*, Stanislavsky came into his own in the more crowded choreography required for Act 3. He opens it with Elena and Sonia playing a piano duet (thus spoiling the symbolism of the silent piano), Voinitsky throwing his hat and overcoat on a chair and conducting the performance, correcting Sonia's wrong notes. When the clock strikes one, Voinitsky checks his watch. During Sonia and Elena's brief exchange Stanislavsky had Sonia on the verge of sobbing, chewing her fingernails, while Elena jerks her hand away from Sonia's lips. In the climax of the act Stanislavsky had all mention of numbers and figures heavily stressed. Voinitsky was to come to the front of the stage and, with his back to the audience, confront Serebriakov. Stanislavsky then crossed out Voinitsky's threatening words, 'You won't forget me' (*Budesh' menia pomnit'*) and after the bungled murder attempt had Voinitsky point the gun at his own forehead, with a ten-second silent freeze before the curtain fell. The same meticulous care and the same need to fiddle with the text is found in Act 4. The care is expressed in the orchestration of non-verbal elements at the end: the cricket chirping, the rain dripping from the roof, the banging of the night-watchman and the guitar climax with heavy rain. Much of Elena's and Astrov's farewell is rearranged, with a long pause inserted in which Elena leans with her elbows against the door frame, as if blocking any exit.

There is one touch that Stanislavsky puts on the last page after his own signature, 'Finished 27 May 1899, K. Alekseev: "And life anyway is stupid, boring," is Chekhov's own phrase.' It suggests how close Astrov is to Chekhov (at least in Stanislavsky's opinion), so that we may well interpret the progression from the Wood Demon to Astrov as representing a disillusion and coarsening in the author's own self.

Nemirovich-Danchenko and his colleagues kept sending telegrams to Yalta, rousing Chekhov from his sickbed, sending him barefoot in the dark to his newly installed telephone. Chekhov was irritated and embarrassed not to have seen the play even in rehearsal, even more by an item in a newspaper: 'A.P. Chekhov, very interested in the staging of his drama *Uncle Vania* by the Artistic-Popular Theatre troupe, has sent a writer-friend a letter asking for details of the staging of *Uncle Vania*.' But to judge by the telegrams Chekhov received, Stanislavsky's production met the same ecstatic audience response as his *Seagull*. Olga Knipper, however, like some of the cast, felt dissatisfied until several performances had taught the actors how to cope with the Chekhovian 'images'. Nemirovich-Danchenko felt that the text itself was still not perfect, that the motivation for Voinitsky's attack on the professor was so obscure that it inhibited audience response. (Later, in his articles, Nemirovich-Danchenko blamed his production for devoting more time to sound effects than the lyrical potential of the text.) Nevertheless, by the sixth performance (10 November 1899) Vishnevsky, who played Voinitsky, could write: 'We acted amazingly today!!! The theatre was crammed to overflowing. I have never known such a reception [...] Groans and shouts filled the theatre! We had fifteen curtain calls.'

Chekhov's rivals went to see it: Gorky, by no means a friend of Chekhovian drama, commented, 'I don't consider the play a pearl, but I see more content in it than others do; its content is enormous, symbolist, and in form it is a completely original, unique thing.' Shortly afterwards (24 January 1900), Tolstoy visited MKhaT. His dairy records, 'I went to see *Uncle Vania* and was indignant.' He is reported to have complained that 'despite brilliant passages there was no tragic situation, that it was pointless to hint at any meaning in the sound of the guitar or of the cricket, that Astrov and Voinitsky were rubbish, idlers, running from action, that they should have married peasant girls and stopped pestering Serebriakov.' The perversity of this response is outrageous when we consider Tolstoy's late drama, particularly *A Living Corpse*, where the best elements are very Chekhovian irrational touches and liberalism.

The success of *Uncle Vania*, performed by professionals and amateurs in the provinces, was unprecedented, so much so that the new director of the Imperial theatres overrode their previous decision and only MKhaT's intervention stopped the Aleksandrinsky theatre from performing it in Petersburg. Effectively, Stanislavsky was acquiring a monopoly of Chekhov in the metropolitan theatre, which Nemirovich-Danchenko defended as 'a defence of Chekhov's artistic interests'. (Nemirovich-Danchenko considered St Petersburg actors, especially in the Maly theatre, as unsuitable for Chekhovian characters because of their incorrigibly handsome voices and rhythms.)

In their letters to Chekhov it is remarkable how unanimously critics agreed that this play was closely linked with *The Seagull* as a basis for a new drama and a 'hammer to beat the public's head'. Likewise, attention focused on Act 4 and the tragic implication that Sonia and Voinitsky now had no future. Chekhov's cousin, Georgi Mitrofanovich, in his letter from

Taganrog spoke for many: 'The tableau of the final act was extraordinarily sad and depressing, it left on all the spectators an impression that was heavier than any tragic scenes.' The reactions were often personal, even intrusive: one MKhaT actor wrote, 'I a man of 22 wept...not only for uncle Vania, for Astrov, but mainly for you. God, how alone you are and how little personal happiness you have. Astrov's notes of universal grief are covered by a heavy chord of lack of love, happiness, personal happiness.' *Uncle Vania* may have been the first major Chekhov play to be performed abroad, for an amateur group of Russians played it in Paris in January 1902.[17] One spectator recorded in her diary, 'amid the merriment and noise of Paris I heard a sound penetrating right into my heart – a voice from the homeland, an echo of its life.' Many of these reactions, optimistic, pessimistic, puzzled or adoring, were addressed to Chekhov and his occasional, if taciturn responses are sometimes illuminating: for instance in one reply to an actress's letter he enlarged on his conception of Elena, 'Perhaps Elena Andreevna may seem incapable of thinking or even loving, but when I was writing *Uncle Vania* I had something quite different in mind.'

Faced with the play's success on stage, the literary critics began to run with the hare, not the hounds. The Moscow critics in particular drifted away from their usual assessments based on sociology and representativeness and began to appreciate novelty as a virtue: 'Mr Chekhov feels, thinks and perceives life in episodes, particulars, in its flotsam and jetsam and, if one may say so, infinite parallels that never intersect, at least, not on any visible plane,' wrote one of his most perceptive critics, Kugel (*Teatr i iskusstvo* [1900] 8, 168-9). In St Petersburg it was the symbolists who were readiest to welcome Chekhov for, as Filosofov put it, 'truly decadent refinement'. (Chekhov was less inclined to read, let alone respond to, professional criticism: 'I don't read such articles so as not to foul my mood' he wrote to Nemirovich-Danchenko [3 xii 99].) However, on 6 November 1899 Rakshanin in the Stock Exchange Gazette (*Birzhevaia gazeta*), usually the most aesthetically inclined of the Petersburg newspapers, took a broader view: 'Until recently playwrights of all countries and times wrote dramas, comedies and vaudevilles for the stage. For these writings there were definite forms, specific requirements, there was a tradition which seemed unshakeable. [...] We are now undoubtedly present at a battle of a new tendency in dramatic writing with the established forms, and Anton Chekhov is at the head of the movement. [...] *Uncle Vania* of course is not a comedy, even less a drama, undoubtedly it is not a vaudeville – it is in fact "a mood in four acts".'

It was not until 10 April 1900, when the MKhaT came to Sevastopol that Chekhov saw his play in production. Stanislavsky records: 'We were moved by the dark figure of the author hidden in the director's box behind the backs of Vl. Nemirovich-Danchenko and his wife. The first act had a chilly reception. By the end success had become a great ovation. The author was called for. He was in despair, but still came forth.' Chekhov went backstage with advice, especially on Astrov. Stanislavsky realised: 'Astrov is a cynic, he has become one from contempt for the vulgarity around him. He isn't sentimental and doesn't sulk...he cancels out the lyricism of Uncle Vania's and Sonia's finale.'

The influence of *Uncle Vania* grew with its reputation; in Germany it clearly affected Arthur Schnitzler, whose play *Der einsame Weg* (*The Lonely Way* [1903]),[18] with its dandy hero Stephan von Sala, stakes his claim to be called the 'German Chekhov'. 'Not much has made such an unforgettable impression on me as *Uncle Vania* in as staged by the Moscow Arts Theatre,' Schnitzler wrote.[19]

In Russia *Uncle Vania* became the least contentious of Chekhov's plays; its relative simplicity, its brevity and economy, the absence of complicated effects and sets made it accessible to provincial repertory and amateur theatre; its title role was easily identifiable with many a spectator's uncle and thus became a byword. Maiakovsky, an unlikely worshipper of Chekhov, argued in his *Two Chekhovs* (1914) that (like the futurists) Chekhov was an innovative artist of words, not ideas: 'Take his bloodless dramas. Behind the stained glass of words life is discernible only as much as is necessary. Where another writer would have needed to use a suicide to justify someone's parading round the stage, Chekhov gives the highest drama in the simple "grey" words: *Astrov*: "But the heat in that Africa there must be really terrific".'

After the revolution Chekhov became an official icon, and provoked reaction not so much against him as against the mummification of his work. Bulgakov satirises *Uncle Vania* in his play *The Days of the Turbins*, where the embattled heroes compete for the attention of an unhappily married Elena: no sooner does the poet-figure declare 'We shall rest' than nine gun-shots belie his hopes. Osip Mandelstam's sketch (1935) for a broadcast[20] on *Uncle Vania* is indignant. It opens with the cast list and then asks: 'Why are they together? [...] Try and define the qualities or kinship of Voinitsky, son of the widow of a privy councillor, of the mother of the professor's first wife, with Sofia Aleksandrovna, the professor's daughter by his first wife. I for one find it easier to understand the funnel-shaped outline of Dante's comedy with its circles, routes and spherical astronomy, than this petty-passport nonsense. A biologist would call the Chekhovian principle ecological. Cohabitation is the determining factor for Chekhov. There is no action in his plays, there is only contiguity and the unpleasant-nesses that result. Chekhov takes a sample with a pipette from a non-existent human "mire". People live together and just cannot separate. That is all.'

In post-Soviet prose, Viacheslav P'etsukh showed the same touching irreverence in his sketch *Uncle Senia*,[21] where the actor of this name has to play Uncle Vania in a provincial performance: 'things were so bad that in the middle of Act 4 Voinitsky, thanks to a whim of the Vologda director, commits suicide.' Pretending to be dead, Uncle Senia snarls at the sufferings of Uncle Vania: 'No, what a life they screwed up, the dogs – it was a fairy tale, not life!'

The very success of *Uncle Vania* has prevented Russian directors from much experimentation – only the Soviet insistence on making Sonia's last speech a prophecy of post-revolutionary bliss temporarily blighted the Chekhovian mood. With the fragmentation of Russia's theatres in the 1990s, however, some experimentation has taken place. Desnitsky's classically minimal production on the tiny stage of the theatre *U nikitskikh vorot* of 1993 contrasts with the Petersburg Maly theatre's attempt (directed by Sergei Soloviov) to prove Nemirovich-Danchenko wrong by assembling the maximum of detail and turning it into a compendium of Chekhoviana, giving Uncle Vania the cello that uncles traditionally play in Russian literature (e.g. in Turgenev's *Fathers and Sons* or Chekhov's *Ivanov*), making Sonia (however unlikely) a secret drinker of vodka like Masha in *The Seagull*, with Sonia's hay-making visible from the house (like the hay in Stanislavsky's production of *The Cherry Orchard*), emphasising the emotional weight behind every mention of the dead Vera Petrovna, amassing detail with an exactitude and fussiness that would amaze even Stanislavsky. *Uncle Vania* also acquired a second life in the Russian cinema. Notable is the 1975 version by Mikhail Konchalovsky in which Bondarchuk plays a rather middle-aged Astrov and Smoktunovsky plays an omni-present Vania, who, when not taking part in the action, is listening to it through the wall from his den of a room, in a house of almost Edgar Allen Poe atmosphere: the mood of brooding depression intensifying to the point of insanity is cinematically powerful, even though it is unfaithful to the callous comic strain of Chekhov's play.

Although Chekhov's second life can be said to be taking place in English, Chekhov's plays met the greatest resistance in England. The London production of *Uncle Vania* in 1914, however, roused *The Times* to commend it as 'a play utterly opposed to all our English notions of play making, a play of will-less people, futile people, drifters, just pottering on with their disappointed, frustrated lives[22]...not Vania, but little Sonia, is its central figure.' Other reviewers condemned it as 'a desolate, dreary, competent piece of work, no doubt good for us to see once...'. Directed by Komisarjevsky in 1921, the next English version of *Uncle Vania* was more successful: 'what Chekhov has done and what nobody else has ever attempted is to put on the stage that which in all other plays happens during the *entr' actes*,' commented Desmond McCarthy in *New Statesman*, while James Agate declared the play 'quite perfect,' a view which long remained challenged, however tragically or comically Chekhov's subtitle 'Scenes from country life' was interpreted. Howard Barker, a radical playwright turned producer, however, has now decided to resolve his 'quarrel with Chekhov a man [...] who has to some extent institutionalised failure' by staging a version of *Uncle Vania* in which Vania shoots straight at the professor, with catastrophic results.[23]

If in Germany *Uncle Vania* found a ready acceptance (until the coming of the Nazis), in France it had to overcome the prejudice of critics such as Schlumberger, who in 1921 declared that the play 'lacked gathering, sacrifice in establishing the plan, it scorns the underlining of action, without which our taste for architecture is unsatisfied.' When Georges Pitoëff (who had studied under Stanislavsky) staged *Uncle Vania* in 1922, however, the view was transformed: Lucien Descaves found it had 'an anguish and an undeniable beauty.' In Japan, after Maurice Baring's chapter on Chekhov's plays had been translated, *Uncle Vania* was singled out for attention, just as in China it became by the 1950s the favourite foreign play.

Not only readers, but theatre performers, have been swayed by the interpretations of literary critics. In the English-speaking world they tended to emphasise the elegiac, melancholy aspects of *Uncle Vania* and played down the farce. Some of the best (and most influential) critiques have come from scholars with no knowledge of Russian; few have equalled the insights of F.L. Lucas in his *The Drama of Chekhov, Synge, Yeats and Pirandello* (London: Cassell, 1963). Although Lucas dismisses *The Wood Demon* out of hand, his identification of *Uncle Vania* and its diatribe against Serebriakov with Chekhov's personal loathing of critics. In such critiques Chekhov's play was pulled out of its Russian context and placed in a wider and larger context of unhappy comedies of love, of sylvan settings destroyed, from Ronsard and Molière to Thomas Hardy and Flaubert, whose god-like Dr Rivière Lucas turns into a Titanic predecessor of the Chekhovian doctor. Such an approach, of course, is open to the accusation that it contradicts Chekhov's own insistence on the comic nature of his work and the critic, like critics of Molière, is forced to take refuge in the notorious phrase 'Then Chekhov [Molière] was wrong.'

Of the linguistically qualified critics in English, David Magarshack (in *Chekhov the Dramatist* [New York: Hill and Wang, 1960]) was the first to deal adequately with the relationship between *The Wood Demon* and *Uncle Vania*. He divides Chekhov's plays into conventional plays of direct action and innovative plays of indirect action; he called *The Wood Demon* a play of transition, and classified *Uncle Vania* as a play of indirect action, setting out in parallel columns at least one scene from Act 1 of each play to show how very similar texts have different impact in changed frameworks. Before Magarshack no critic had given *The Wood Demon* such a fair examination. Magarshack emphasises the complete opposition of Chekhov's intentions and achievement: 'teeming with coincidences and *deus ex machina* situations [...] the action of the play is in fact full of unlife-like melodramatic touches.'

Maurice Valency attracted attention to his study of Chekhov's drama by the serendipity of his title, *The Breaking String* (New York: Oxford University Press, 1966). He gave the first coherent account in English of the genesis of *The Wood Demon* and rightly points out that the play's contemporary critics never objected to the worst faults of the play: the use of 'found' letters and diaries to make the plot and hasten its dénouement. Valency is a loyal Chekhovian in insisting that *Uncle Vania's* 'comedic aspects are quite incompatible with a tragic action' and sees the play as an ambiguous drama in which all the characters are mentally ill and 'have wrapped themselves up more or less comfortably against the elemental blasts'. The critical complacency becomes questionable only when Valency concludes that *Uncle Vania* shows 'Chekhov had achieved a certain proficiency in this exacting medium' (whereas 'the *Three Sisters* is not a well-made play. It is a chronicle in which may be discerned only the vestiges of a plot.')

Other critics such as J.L. Styan (*Chekhov in Performance: A Commentary on the Major Plays* [Cambridge University Press, 1971]) have directed their efforts not so much towards a reader's interpretation but a director's staging. Styan is anxious that the director should appreciate the agrarian poverty of the world outside Chekhov's sets. Otherwise, too, this is an interpretation that centres on political issues: an interesting poll is produced to show how critics and directors of all nations split almost evenly on whether to interpret Sonia's last speech as a call for optimism or an illusion born of despair. The concern for consensus forces Styan to relegate his best insights to footnotes, notably a comment that the end of Act 2, in which Astrov and Sonia negotiate their future non-relationship foreshadows Act 4 of *The Cherry Orchard* and the even bleaker scene between Varia and Lopakhin.

The next generation of critics, such as Richard Peace (*Chekhov: A Study of the Four Major Plays* [Yale: Harvard University Press, 1983]) and Laurence Senelick (*Modern Dramatists: Anton Chekhov* [London: Macmillan, 1985]) have paid less attention to Chekhov's development as a whole and have treated *Uncle Vania* as a work in the modern canon. Peace pays special attention to the almost Japanese role of the tea-drinking around which Act 1 is constructed and investigates the symbolism of the names, Voinitsky representing the 'warring' principle (*voin-*) and Elena the principle of idleness (*len'-*). Senelick has been more concerned to integrate *Uncle Vania* with modern, especially French drama (Beckett). Senelick points out the Bergsonian nature of Chekhovian time, as a flow outside which the characters are unable to stand, imprisoned like Proust in subjective time. The play thus becomes more like a novel, for time, it is implied in Chekhovian drama, must go on flowing after the curtain-fall. Senelick has fewer insights into the genesis of Chekhov's work than Russian critics, but his is one of the best attempts to fit it into the 20th-century European Zeitgeist, to see its link to the desolate symbolism of Strindberg. Perhaps the tendency to recruit Chekhov posthumously into the Theatre of the Absurd has gone too far; as the German critic Maria Deppermann has pointed out in a number of articles (see Kluge, op. cit., pp. 1161-86). *Uncle Vania* opens and closes with scenes of human affection which are completely uncharacteristic of the absurd and the alienated. However hopeless, Sonia's consolation of Vania and, however uncomprehending, Marina's concern for Astrov affirm some sort of sense and communion in human life.

A Concluding Word

Our commentary on *The Wood Demon* partly forecloses any conclusion: a miraculous transformation into *Uncle Vania* has applied the experimental results of *The Seagull* to what anyone would have thought an intractably bad abortive comedy. A genre of cruel comedy has been perfected. Nevertheless, Chekhov's plays are not only a linear progression to ever more sure-footed, complex and ambiguous modernist comedy. *Uncle Vania* has features which are unique: of all Chekhov's plays it is least indebted to others' work. There is none of the Maupassant allusion that haunts *The Seagull* or *The Cherry Orchard*; even the universal Shakespearean Hamlet element is limited to Voinitsky's dependence on provoking his mother, his hatred of Serebriakov's usurpation and his pointlessly belated violent action. Music plays a smaller part than in any of Chekhov's major plays: we have seen how the operatic allusions are cut and the piano remains silent – only Telegin's guitar remains. Because it was written, as a sculpture is chiselled, by removing unnecessary material, rather than by building up a structure, *Uncle Vania* is a much more focused play than the two major works that follow. It can be reduced to a moral, an illustration of what Sonia blurts out as Elena sets out to save or wreck her hopes: 'No, not knowing [*neizvestnost'*] is better.' The ending is the pain of knowledge which will be too strong for the mystical analgesic that Sonia improvises.

The dating of Chekhov's major remoulding of *The Wood Demon* is confirmed by the way in which it takes devices first used in *The Seagull* a step further towards the last two plays. The lessons of *The Seagull*, both positive and negative, are applied in the writing of *Uncle Vania*. The positive lessons are in the economy of characterisation and above all in the symbolism. The rivalry of Treplev and Trigorin has coloured the irrational hatred of Voinitsky for the professor; Sonia, with her faith against all the evidence in the need to battle on, has acquired elements of Nina; above all, fewer characters have more roles thrust upon them, and in this lies the new Chekhovian economy. The symbolism of birds so rich in *The Wood Demon* and in *The Seagull* is cut: no longer do the screech owl, hawks and eagles, to which the characters of *The Wood Demon* are compared and which form the symbols of Treplev's miniature play, roam freely in the play. They are now part of a death list: just as all creatures are doomed to extinction in

Treplev's play about the remote future, so the elk, duck and geese are now confined to the commemoration of the extinct in Astrov's sets of maps. Symbolism is concentrated into episodes framed by the main action. Literary allusion has been cut to a minimum; characters no longer read or quote books on stage.

But the art of the obsessive monologue as seduction is arguably developed from Trigorin's speech to Nina into Astrov's lecture to Elena. Likewise, irrelevant music replaces the only too obviously relevant Tchaikovsky of earlier dramatic technique. Treplev's waltz and the music across the lake in counterpoint to Masha's misery paves the way for Telegin's cruelly cheerful strumming and polkas. A cruel outside world, whether the stepmother and the provincial theatre of *The Seagull* or the diseased peasantry of *Uncle Vania*, replace the sunlit rural paradise of the earlier play. The setting in one house (unlike the alternations of *Ivanov* and *The Wood Demon*), introduces an atmosphere of confinement so important to the late Chekhov. Above all, an all-pervading irony, where the stage directions and the situation give the lie to any affirmation the characters may care to end with, create the new genre of cruel comedy. Sonia's 'Not knowing is better – there is still hope' is now given the lie, for we are now told everything about the future, if far less about the past. Here Chekhov's drama is the polar opposite of Ibsen's. In rewriting his play, Chekhov has moved it into a new genre, the cruel comedy of the 20th century.

But there is a gentler side to *Uncle Vania* which distinguishes it from *The Seagull* and *The Cherry Orchard* and aligns it with *Three Sisters*. It is not subtitled comedy by the author. The endings of *Uncle Vania* and *Three Sisters* both reach out to an audience's sympathy for undeserving, stoical provincial victims of metropolitan (or military) rapacity; like the three sisters, Astrov, Sonia and Vania are gathering strength and faith to face an unredeemably bleak future. For this reason alone the two plays brought Chekhov a torrent of letters of appreciation from provincial audiences who were grateful for what they saw as the first public representation of their predicament and their goodness. No other Chekhov plays met with such a widespread extra-literary response. Like *Three Sisters*, *Uncle Vania* is a play about bereavement: the central characters are cut off from light by the shadow of their beloved dead; Vera Petrovna, the real love of her brother Voinitsky, has paralysed everyone by her death, just as the death of Colonel Prozorov, who has made the three sisters, leaves them eternally incapable of action. *Uncle Vania* as a play on the dire and prolonged consequences of bereavement continues to strike a subconscious chord in the audience, and that note cancels out the callousness of the authorial irony. The role of the absent and of the silent is perhaps what we have so far least understood in Chekhovian drama; it is difficult for a critic or a spectator fully to account for what has not been said or done in the drama, and in *Uncle Vania* the 'dog that did not bark in the night' is as significant as the dog that did. We have noted the dramatic importance of the silence between Sonia and Elena that endures for the first half of the play; we might also note that Marina, that unshakeable rock of ages, may console Astrov, Telegin, Serebriakov and Sonia, but that she never interacts with Elena or Uncle Vania; her non-communication implies their isolation, even their moral foundering. The economy of Chekhov's art, perfected in *Uncle Vania*, lies in the significant omission whose impact on the audience goes direct to the subconscious.

Tables 1-4

Stanislavsky's mise-en-scène (sketched after Stanislavsky's drawings).

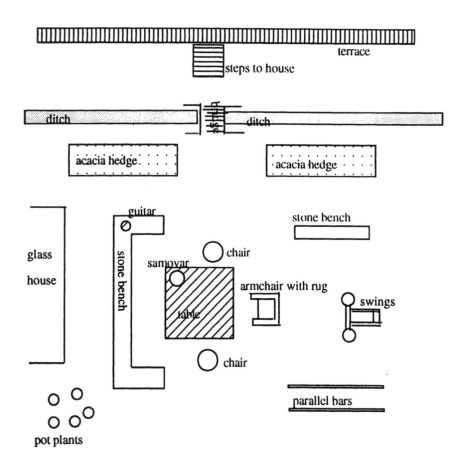

Stanislavsky's set for Act 1 of *Uncle Vania*.

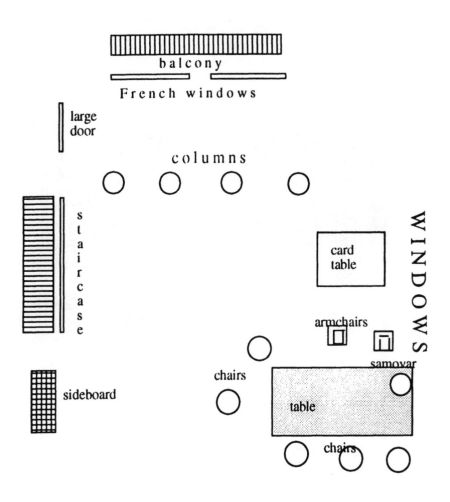

Stanislavsky's set for Act 2 of *Uncle Vania*.

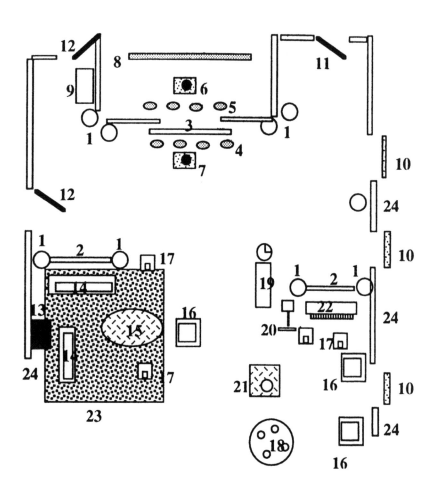

Stanislavsky's set for Act 3 of *Uncle Vania.*

Key
1 columns; 2 trellis; 3 glass; 4, 5 flower baskets; 6, 7 flower beds with Chinese vase; 8 backdrops; 9 modern cupboard; 10 3 stained glass windows with red curtains; 11 door to garden; 12 doors to rest of house; 13 stove; 14 sofas; 15 table; 16 covered armchairs; 17 covered chairs; 18 covered candelabra; 19 grandfather clock; 20 music stand; 21 card table with jug of water; 22 upright piano; 23 carpet; 24 walls with eight family portraits.

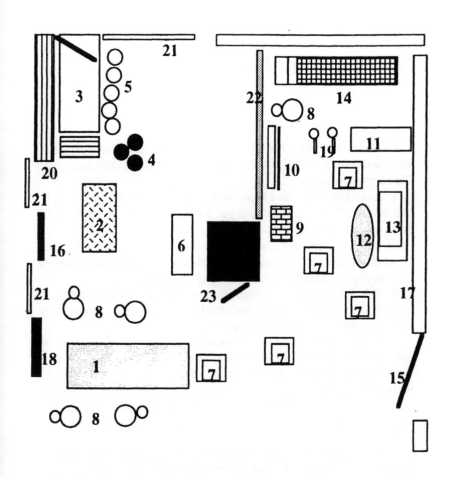

Stanislavsky's set for Act 4 of *Uncle Vania*.

Key
1 table with office books, inkwells, abacus, lamp; 2 small table, maps, 2 candles; 3 entry door (raised), boarded, papered screen, hung with horse harness, whips, rope; 4 weights; 5 sacks; 6 cupboard, ledgers; 7 leather armchairs; 8 plain wooden chairs; 9 iron trunk; 10 bookcase; 11 chest of drawers, guns, hunting stuff; 12 oilcloth covered table; 13 leather sofa; 14 bed with sheet and blanket; 15 door to yard; 16 map of Africa; 17 a few portraits; 18 map-making materials; 19 lamps; 20 shelves; 21 windows; 22 screen; 23 open stove (alight).

Notes to Part Two

1. The only comparable case is the abandonment and subsequent transformation of the story *A Visit to Friends [U znakomykh]* of 1898 into a play, *The Cherry Orchard*.

2. It is curious that when Menshikov saw the play in 1901, he failed to take offence: 'I'm very grateful to you for the professor – an exposure of that type is long overdue,' he wrote to Chekhov.

3. It is interesting that Chekhov knew Stevenson's story *Dr Jekyll and Mr Hyde* and possible that the satanic streaks in the doctors in Chekhov's later plays owe something to his reading of Stevenson.

4. This joke is best represented by a *New Yorker* cartoon in which an amazed woman listens to a man in a hotel lobby: he is saying, 'No, you stay down here and I'll fetch my etchings.'

5. See Simon Karlinsky, *Huntsmen, Birds, Forests, and Three Sisters* in Jean-Pierre Barricelli, *Chekhov's Great Plays* (New York, 1981) 144-60.

6. Telegin's attempts at a red herring, his reference to his brother-in-law who is a Master of Arts, is one of several lines salvaged from Act 4 of *The Wood Demon*.

7. I am indebted to Harai Golomb, *A Badenweiler View of Chekhov's Endings* (in R.D. Kluge, *Čechov...*, see Bibliography) for many of the ideas in this chapter.

8. Note how the bird imagery grows out of Act 4, Scene 1 of *The Wood Demon* where Elena is compared to a canary and a sparrow, and Sonia talks of her pet canary whose top notes are false. To the bird imagery we can add Maria Vasilievna described as a jackdaw in both plays. Unlike the Wood Demon, Astrov compares himself not to an eagle, but to an old sparrow (in Act 3); Elena's poetic avian image is also demoted by Astrov when he calls her 'a predatory furry polecat.'

9. In *The Cherry Orchard*, too, Kharkov, with its inhabitants longing for country cottages on the former orchard, is linked with decline and corruption: the overtones of *kharkat'* (to clear one's throat) doubtless affect Chekhov's reaction to the city more than any real geographical factor.

10. All Chekhov's plays are indebted to Turgenev's *A Month in the Country* (which was almost unperformed in the 19th century). *Uncle Vania* is, however, particularly close to Turgenev's play, not just in situation but in such details as the stage directions: for a fine analysis, see A.D. Briggs,

'Two Months in the Country', in Irene Zohrab (ed.), *Festschrift for Patrick Waddington* (Wellington, New Zealand, forthcoming).

11. In Stanislavsky's production this mundane tally of years is stylised: Voinitsky calculates his remaining years of life on the abacus as if he were accounting for his peas and curds.

12. 'Freud would have enjoyed the revealing quality of his last pathetic proposal that Yelena should give herself to him in the depths of the forest.' Eric Bentley, *In Search of Theater* (New York, 1954) 349.

13. Chekhov marked this part of the document in pencil with an irritated 'On whose part?' [*U kogo?*] As he was to insist to Olga Knipper, who not for the last time showed disappointing perversity in interpreting her roles; Astrov was not passionate towards Elena, but idly lecherous.

14. In 1899, however, the Aleksandrinsky theatre in St Petersburg tried and failed to secure the play and override the Committee's ban.

15. The power of Stanislavsky's acting may explain why some spectators felt that Astrov, not Voinitsky, should be the title role, that the centre of gravity had not really shifted from the doctor to Voinitsky in the conversion of *The Wood Demon* into *Uncle Vania*.

16. I am very grateful to the curator and archivist of the Museum of MKhaT in Moscow for permission to study this copy. It is numbered 18890, and dated 27 May 1899, with additional notes for Acts 1 in Nemirovich-Danchenko's hand (in red and blue). As the copy awaits publication I have agreed to restrain from a comprehensive description of Stanislavsky's annotations and have limited myself to a few quotations and to a rough reproduction of Stanislavsky's sketches for the sets. Stanislavsky had unsewn a copy of Chekhov's *Plays* (1897) and for every page of Chekhov's text of *Uncle Vania* he interleaved a page of notes before rebinding the play. Most of Stanislavsky's many additional stage directions were not incorporated into Chekhov's next edition of the work (1901). It is clear, however, that the few changes in the final version of *Uncle Vania* in Chekhov's collected works stem mostly from Stanislavsky's alterations.

17. There were, however, several performances in Czech in Prague and the Bohemian provinces in 1901.

18. Schnitzler's play was performed in Russian in MKhaT on the same night in 1904 as *Uncle Vania* was first performed in the Künstlertheater in Vienna.

19. See Maria Deppermann, *Tschechov und Arthur Schnizler*, in Kluge, op. cit., pp. 1161-85.

20. The talk was never broadcast: see Osip Mandelstam, *Sobranie sochinenii IV* (Paris, 1981) 107-9.

21. Viachelsav P'etsukh, *Tsikly* (Moscow, 1991) 155-61.

22. A sentence repeated almost verbatim in another unsigned review of the play in *The Times* in 1945.

23. *The Guardian* (9 April 1994) 29.

Select Bibliography

Primary sources

including *The Wood Demon*

Chekhov, Anton Pavlovich, *Polnoe sobranie sochinenii* (Moscow: Nauka, 1978) vols 12-13.

Koteliansky, S.S. (transl.), *Chekhov, Plays and Stories* (London: Dent, 1937).

Hingley, Ronald Chekhov (transl.), *Chekhov, Uncle Vania, The Cherry Orchard and The Wood Demon* (Oxford: Oxford University Press, 1974, 1989).

not including *The Wood Demon*

Frayn, Michael (transl.), *Chekhov, Plays* (London/New York: Methuen, 1993).

Secondary sources

for a fuller bibliography up to the mid-1980s, the reader is referred to:

Wellek, R. & N., *Chekhov: New Perspectives* (Englewood Cliffs, N.J.: Prentice Hall, 1984) 199-200.

Clyman, Toby W., *A Chekhov Companion* (Westport/London: Greenwood Press, 1985) 310-31.

Worrall, Nick, *File on Chekhov* (London: Methuen, 1986).

1. Critiques

Abdullaeva, Z., 'Doktor Astrov i drugie', *Literaturnoe obozrenie* (1985) 11, 87-90.

Barricelli, Jean-Pierre (ed.), *Chekhov's Great Plays* (New York: New York University Press, 1981).

Bordinat, P., *Dramatic structure in Uncle Vania*, 47-60.

Kovitz, S., *A Fine Day to Hang Oneself*, 189-200.

Vitins, I., *Uncle Vania's Predicaments*, 35-46.

Chudakov, A., *Mir Chekhova* (Moscow: Sovetsky pisatel', 1986).

Clayton, Douglas, 'Chekhov's *Diadia Vania* and the Traditional Comic Structure', *Russian Language Journal* 40 (1986) 103-10.

Czerwinski, E.J., 'Chekhov Reconstructed', *Slavic & E. European Arts* (1986) 4, 7-18.

Dolotova A.M., 'Zachem srubili berezniak i sosnovy bor? Ot Naivnogo leshego k *Diade Vane*', in V.Ia. Lakshin (ed.), *Chekhoviana* (Moscow: Nauka, 1990) 83-90.

Dubnova E.Ia., '*Diadia Vania* na stsene peterburgskogo Dramaticheskogo teatra V.F. Komissarzhevskoi', in V.Ia. Lakshin (ed.), *Chekhoviana (III)* (Moscow: Nauka, 1993) 117-29.

Emeljanow, Victor, *Komisarjevsky directs Chekhov in London* (Theatre Notebook, 1983) 37, 66-77.

Karas', A.. 'Leshii, koldun, obmanshchik i svat', *Moskovski nabliudatel'*, (1993) 11-12, 30-3.

Kingsbury, Stewart A., 'Name Symbolism in Chekhov's *Uncle Vania*', in *Festschrift in Honor of Virgil J. Vogel* (DeKalb: Illinois Name Soc., 1985) 46-58.

Kuzicheva, A.P., 'Liubil li Chekhov teatr', *Voprosy teatra* (Moscow: Rossiiskii institut iskusstvoznaniia, 1993) 13, 116-37.

Kluge R-D. (ed.), *Čechov: Werk und Wirkung*, 2 vols (Wiesbaden, Germany: Opera Slavica, 1990).

Allain, Louis, *Teatral'naia semiotika A. P. Chekhova*, 254-63.

Babović, Miloslav, *Psikhologizm v sisteme motivirovki p'es Chekhova*, 395-406.

Christa, Boris, *Vestimentary Markers in Chekhov's Play*, 182-92.

Golomb, Harai, *A Badenweiler View of Chekhov's Endings*, 232-53.

Kšicová, Danuše, *Stil' modern v dramaturgii A. P. Chekhova*, 777-90.

Levin, Viktor D., *Nekotorye cherty iazykovoi struktury dialoga v dramaturgii Chekhova*, 208-20.

Senderovich, Saveli, *Anton Chekhov and St George the Dragonslayer*, 543-72.

Loritto, O., 'Kstati, o ptichkakh', *Moskovski nabliudatel'* (1993) 11-12, 78-9.

McVay, Gordon, 'Chekhov in Britain 1990', *Scottish Slavonic Review* (1991) 16, 103-5.

Maiakovski, V., 'Dva Chekhova', in *Polnoe sobranie sochinenii 1* (Moscow: Khudlit, 1955) 294-301.

Miles, Patrick, *Chekhov on the British Stage* (England: Sam & Sam, 1987).

Peace, Richard, *Chekhov: A Study of the Four Major Plays* (New Haven: Yale University Press, 1983).

Rozanova, Evgeniia, 'Pomianut li nas dobrym slovom', *Teatr* (Moscow, 1993) 3, 70-5.

Senelick, L., *Modern Dramatists: Anton Chekhov* (London: Macmillan, 1983).

Soloviova, I., 'Milaia sestra. *Diadia Vania* v Malom teatre', *Moskovski nabliudatel'*, (1993) 11-12, 40-3.

Styan, J.L., *Chekhov in Performance: A Commentary on the Major Plays* (Cambridge: Cambridge University Press, 1971).

Zverev, A., 'Iavlenie i chelovek: *Diadia Vania* na segodniashnei stsene', *Literaturnoe obozrenie* (1984) 3, 95-7.

2. Biographies

Gitovich, N.I., *Letopis' zhizni i tvorchestva A.P. Chekhova* (Moscow: Khudlit, 1955).

Hingley, Ronald, *A New Life of Anton Chekhov* (Oxford: Oxford University Press, 1976).

Kuzicheva, A.P., *Vash Chekhov (1892-1898)*, in *Soglasie* (Moscow, 1992) 6-12; (1993) 1-6.

Magarshack, David, *Stanislavsky – A Life* (London: Faber & Faber, 1986).

Pritchett, V.S., *Chekhov: A Biography* (London: Penguin Books, 1990).

Rayfield, Donald, *Chekhov: A Life* (London: Harper Collins [forthcoming, 1996]).

Simmons, E.J., *Chekhov, a biography* (London: Cape, 1963).

Troyat, Henri, *Chekhov* (London: Macmillan, 1987).

Vinogradskaia, I., *Zhizn' i tvorchestvo K.S. Stanislavskogo Letopis' v 4i tomakh* (Moscow: Vserossiiskoe teatral'noe obshchestvo, 1971).

Index

Other books available in the series:

Chekhov's *Three Sisters* by G. McVay
Dostoyevsky's *Notes from Underground* by R. Peace
Pushkin's *Queen of Spades* by N. Cornwell
Tolstoy's *Childhood* by G. Williams

forthcoming:

Blok's *The Twelve* by J. Doherty
Gogol's *The Government Inspector* by M. Beresford
Gorky's *Lower Depths* by A. Barratt
Lermontov's *A Hero of our Time* by R. Reid
Pushkin's *The Bronze Horseman* by A. Kahn
Turgenev's *Fathers and Sons* by J. Woodward
Zamyatin's *We* by R. Russell